the spirituaLity of tHe cross

the
spirituality
of the CROSS

The Way of the First Evangelicals

GENE EDWARD VEITH, JR.

CONCORDIA PUBLISHING HOUSE

Copyright © 1999 Concordia Publishing House
3558 S. Jefferson Avenue, St. Louis, MO 63118-3968
Manufactured in the United States of America

Library of Congress Cataloging-in-Publication Data

Veith, Gene Edward, 1951-
      The spirituality of the cross : the way of the first evangelicals /
  Gene Edward Veith, Jr.
          p.   cm.
      Includes bibliographical references.
      ISBN 0-570-05321-8
      1. Spirituality—Lutheran Church. 2. Lutheran Church—Doctrines. I. Title.
  BX8065.2.V45   1999
  230'.41—dc   98-54166

5 6 7 8 9 10 11   09 08 07 06 05 04 03 02

To Pastor Don Kirchhoff,
who brought us in

contents

introduction

Many of us are searching for some kind of a spiritual life, even though we are not always clear about what that means. We yearn for a sense of transcendence, and yet we always come crashing down to earth. The various mysticisms make grandiose promises of enlightenment and spiritual empowerment, but there is no living happily ever after. Mundane life intrudes. Work, family pressures, practical responsibilities, hurting, and failures all have a way of breaking the spiritual mood.

Churches would seem to be custodians of spiritual reality, but they often do not seem particularly spiritual. They often seem mundane too. The whole round of preachers, sitting in the pew, going to fellowship dinners can seem so ordinary. One would think that spirituality would be rather more spectacular.

At least that has been my experience. At different times in my life I have embraced liberal theology, accepting whatever is progressive and crusading for social justice, and I have been a raving, miracle-expecting fundamentalist. My liberalism proved spiritually vacuous, while my fundamentalism proved shallow. I have sat *zazen*, until I found the most that Buddhism promises, namely, emptiness. Mysticism and activism were both bitter disappointments.

What I needed was a spiritual framework big enough to embrace the whole range of human existence, a realistic spirituality. I needed a spirituality that is not a negation of the physical world or ordinary life, but one that transfigures them.

I found it in Christianity, a religion that is not about God as such, but about God in the flesh, and God on the cross. There are many varieties of Christianity, many spiritual traditions within this one historical faith, but they all hinge around this mystery of incarnation, atonement, and redemption.

C. S. Lewis, a major influence on my faith, wrote about "mere Christianity," focusing on what all Christian theologies have in common. This lowest common denominator, he said, was like a hallway, a vestibule from the outside into the house of faith. He went on to point out, however, that to actually live in Christianity, one must leave the hallway and enter one of the rooms. "It is in the rooms, not in the hall, that there are fires and chairs and meals."[1] That is to say, Christians must join some church.

This is where some of the frustrations come. In my own case, none of the local congregations I knew quite measured up to the Christianity I had discovered in books. Part of this was sheer immaturity on my part. Many Christians are often disappointed in actual churches because they hold to impossible ideals and have an inadequate theology of ordinary life. As Lewis says elsewhere, new Christians often think of the church in terms of togas and sandals, rather than everyday human beings like themselves.[2] But it is sometimes true that those "rooms" in the house of Christianity lack fires and chairs and meals.

Each of the varieties of Christianity represents some spiritual tradition, an emphasis or distinctive teaching. It would be naïve to deny that each also has its problems and distortions. This is where the search for Christian spirituality often runs aground.

Another rather ironic problem today is that many of these traditions, however valuable, are now hard to find. The diverse Christian traditions—such as those of Aquinas, Calvin, Wesley— all very different but bracing in their own ways, have been merging into a single generic pop Christianity. It is as if many of Lewis's rooms turn out to be not different at all, serving the same styrofoam-packed fast food, playing the same Muzak, with the same plastic flowers and shag carpeting. This new popularized Christianity seems bland and one-dimensional, full of good feelings, but rather empty of content. In the meantime, the riches and insights of the historical Christian traditions are all but forgotten.

This book is about one of those Christian spiritual traditions, one in which I finally satisfied my own longing for a relationship with God. This book is an introduction to the Lutheran spiritual tradition. This is a faith particularly centered in the cross of Jesus Christ, one that offers a framework for embracing, in an honest and comprehensive way, the whole range of the spiritual life, and whose insights have a profound resonance in ordinary, everyday life.

THE ORIGINAL EVANGELICALS

A better term for "Lutheran" spirituality is "evangelical" spirituality. The term "evangelical" is simply a term derived from the
Greek word for "Gospel," which in turn literally means "good
news." "Evangelical" means someone who focuses on the Gospel of
Jesus Christ, the good news that Christ, through His death and resurrection, has won forgiveness for sinful human beings and offers
salvation as a free gift.

Today the term "evangelical" is used to refer to a wide variety of
more-or-less conservative Protestants. For all of their differences,
Baptists, charismatics, Calvinists, Wesleyans, and the various non-
denominational "para-church ministries" do stress salvation
through Christ and emphasize "evangelism," so the term is apt. But
originally, the word "evangelical" meant "Lutheran."

In the years following the Reformation, "evangelicals" were
those who followed Luther, as opposed to "reformed," who followed Calvin. (A later attempt to bring the two factions together
resulted in the "Evangelical and Reformed Church," today an
American denomination.) Even today in Europe, churches that
follow a Lutheran theology call themselves not "Lutheran"—a
term Luther himself hated, not wanting Christ's Church to be
named after him—but "Evangelical." The American usage of the
term for any Bible-believing, salvation-preaching Christian is
starting to catch on in Europe also, but American tourists at times
get confused when they go into a German or Scandinavian church
with "evangelische" on the sign, expecting revival songs and altar
calls, only to find chorales and liturgy.

Though others are entitled to call themselves "evangelicals,"
Lutherans are at least the first evangelicals. Keeping in mind the
fact that Christians have always focused on the Gospel, from the
New Testament days through the early Church and even through

the Middle Ages—a time when, Protestants contend, the emphasis on the Gospel and its implications became somewhat confused—Lutherans were the first to be *called* evangelical. They were also the first to emphasize the Gospel to such an extent that it became central to every level of their doctrine and practice. This evangelical focus, made over against medieval Catholicism, opened the door to every other Protestant expression that came later. But evangelical Lutheranism remains distinct.

As something of a spiritual wanderer—drifting from religion to religion, church to church, from the very liberal to the very conservative—I myself finally discovered the Gospel. Going deeper and deeper into that Gospel and its implications, I found that I had become a Lutheran. This book is partly a record of that pilgrimage, but only partly. It is mainly an account of what I—as a modern or perhaps post-modern American—have found to be of inestimable help and value in the Lutheran spiritual tradition.

This tradition has been somewhat obscured and is little known in the United States—sometimes, I regret to say, even among American Lutherans—but deserves consideration. Among other reasons, the teachings of the first evangelicals prove to be particularly relevant to problems that are now vexing American Christianity, and they speak in a powerful way to the needs and cravings of today's generations.

SPIRITUALITY AND THEOLOGY

This book is about "spirituality," not theology as such. On one level, this is a misleading distinction. Many people today say that they are not interested in religion, with its doctrines, creeds, and institutions, but they are very interested in "spirituality." They are in the market for something that will give them a pleasant mystical experience and a sense of meaning and well-being, without making any uncomfortable demands on their minds, behavior, or social position. They want religious experience, without religious belief.

Those who see spirituality in terms only of subjective gratification with nothing to do with objective truth lay themselves open to every kind of superstition and exploitation, to every flying-saucer cult and expensive New Age seminar. The fact is, there can be no spirituality without theology, no religious experience apart from religious belief. Even the flying-saucer cults and New Age seminars are selling not only a mystical jolt but a worldview, implicit assumptions about the nature of reality that underlie their messages.

So by "spirituality," I do not mean any kind of content-free, theologically-vacuous quest for transcendent experiences for their own sake. Rather, "spirituality" has to do precisely with the content, what fills abstract theology, mundane institutions, and the everyday life of the Christian with their real substance.

The quest for this kind of spirituality is, I think, genuine and important. Many people today, in our shallow, mass-produced, materialistic culture, yearn for depth, for richness, for transcendence. Many do not even find spiritual substance in their churches, many of which have adopted the slick superficialities and manipulative commercialism of American pop culture, mutating into what can only be described as pop-Christianity. Interestingly, many casualties of pop-Christianity are drifting into older faiths that do seem to offer a measure of spiritual substance. A huge exodus is taking place from Protestantism into the Roman Catholic Church and, perhaps even more significantly, into Eastern Orthodoxy.

Now the notion that Protestantism lacks a vital tradition of the inner spiritual life is simply not true, as this book will show. It is true, however, that American culture—especially today's media-driven pop culture—has made that Protestant spiritual legacy to be nearly forgotten. Exploring an older and far-less Americanized theological and spiritual tradition should prove helpful for Christians trying to keep their bearings. Evangelicals of every kind should profit from going back to their roots, to uncovering the legacy of the First Evangelicals.

For some reason, Lutherans tend to be uncomfortable with proselytizing, with "stealing sheep" from one church to another, and this is really not my intention in writing this book. I think any Christian could draw on the spiritual insights of the Lutheran tradition that will be described here, though of course there will be points of disagreement. But certainly Calvin, for example, has had an influence far beyond the Presbyterian bodies that are formally committed to his teachings, shaping the practice of Baptists and others, many of which take issue with him on particular points while still acknowledging many of his insights. Luther could similarly be useful to a wide range of church bodies. When Christians today struggle with such issues as the role of the church in politics, the use of Scripture, how to live in a sinful world, and how to deal with suffering, Luther—who addressed these issues with penetrating insights—deserves his say. The full dose of Lutheran spirituality can only, of course, be found within the day-to-day life of a Lutheran church.

It should also be emphasized that I am writing as a layman, and am neither a theologian nor a pastor. My approach will be to explain what I have gained from the Lutheran tradition that I have found helpful in my own spiritual life, in terms I hope my fellow ordinary folk will understand. Though the emphasis on spirituality will by no means avoid theology, I will be avoiding most of the technical language, proof-texting, historical analysis, and polemics against other positions that a full-blown work of theology needs to do. I will say almost nothing about the life and times of

Martin Luther, as fascinating as that subject is. Lutherans are strongly grounded in history, but some people have the impression that this faith rests on Luther rather than Christ. The concepts this book will explore have just as much relevance to the 21st century as to the 16th century—possibly more, since the spiritual emptiness of our present age gives them an even sharper edge. I do not even plan to argue for these positions, at least not much; nor do I plan to attack the alternative theologies, nor to defend my own. I will simply lay out what Lutheran spirituality is. The reader can take it or leave it, but at least will come away with a clearer view of a great Christian tradition.

To be sure, technical theology, biblical research, and polemical arguments against contrary views are extraordinarily important, even crucial. One of the great strengths of the Lutheran tradition is that theology is taken seriously and has been thoroughly worked out. Sophisticated theology, biblical scholarship, and vigorous polemics are to be found in abundance among Lutherans. I will provide references to some of these rich theological resources for those who wish to explore the points raised in this book more deeply, to see their scriptural foundation and how they engage other views. But this is not my vocation (a notion that will be made clearer later). Above all, those who want to go deeper can consult with a Lutheran pastor, a vocation and an office that can minister the "cure of souls" in a concrete way, which is more than reading any book. Spirituality, after all, must be lived, not merely intellectualized, and its locus is the mysteries taking place in an ordinary local church.

NOTES

[1] C. S. Lewis, *Mere Christianity* (New York: Macmillan, 1958), xi.
[2] See C. S. Lewis, *Screwtape Letters* (New York: Macmillan, 1961), 12.

justification

THE DYNAMICS OF SIN AND GRACE

Whether in the world's organized religions or in the individual strivings of human beings to find meaning in their lives, certain patterns keep emerging. Adolf Koeberle notes three kinds of spiritual aspiration: moralism, in which the will seeks to achieve perfection of conduct; speculation, in which the mind seeks to achieve perfection of understanding; and mysticism, in which the soul seeks to achieve perfection by becoming one with God.[1] Though all of these ways contain elements of wisdom, Lutheran spirituality is totally different from them all.

Instead of insisting that human beings attain perfection, Lutheran spirituality begins by facing up to imperfection. We cannot perfect our conduct, try as we might. We cannot understand

God through our own intellects. We cannot become one with God. Instead of human beings having to do these things, Lutheran spirituality teaches that God does them for us—He becomes one with us in Jesus Christ; He reveals Himself to our feeble understandings by His Word; He forgives our conduct and, in Christ, lives the perfect life for us.

We do not have to ascend to God; rather, the good news is that He has descended to us. Most philosophies and theologies focus on what human beings must do to be saved; Lutherans insist that there is nothing we can do, but that God does literally everything.

Human sin and God's grace are the two poles of Lutheran spirituality. To be sure, these are intrinsic to all of Christianity, but in Lutheranism they are both heightened. They are resolved in the principle by which, it is said, the church stands or falls: justification by grace through faith.

PATHS TO GOD

The various approaches to the spiritual life cited by Koeberle deserve some more attention, so that the Lutheran perspective can be thrown in higher relief.

The way of moralism seeks to earn God's favor, or a satisfying life, through the achievement of moral perfection—always doing what is right, avoiding wrongdoing of every kind, keeping oneself under control by sheer willpower and a scrupulous conscience. Certainly, the desire to be good is a laudable sentiment—if it only could be accomplished.

Many people assume that moralism is, in fact, what Christianity is all about. Good people go to heaven, it is thought, while bad people go to hell. Christians are those who live morally upright lives, avoiding "sins" while doing good works. Sometimes this takes the form of rather small lifestyle choices—avoiding alcohol, tobacco, and other petty pleasures—while sometimes it takes the form of working for vast ideals, righting the wrongs of society through political activism and social reform.

It is true that some versions of Christianity do tend towards the moralistic. Certainly, moralism characterizes many of the world's religions. In Islam, every detail of life—including the food one eats, the details of family life, and the policies of govern-ment—is regulated by strict moral rules. Even non-religious peo-ple often follow the path of moralism. Animal rights activists, environmentalists, and political activists tend to be just as zealous, perfectionistic, and all-demanding as the most conservative reli-gionist.

Moralism, however, involves a host of impossibilities and con-tradictions. People just do not—and, it seems, cannot—live up to their own high standards. We keep failing. Sometimes, our very attempts at moral perfection lead us to immoral actions, as when our strict rules cause us to hate, coerce, and feel superior to oth-ers. Other times, our own interior attitudes undermine our virtu-ous actions. I myself have done "good works" for which I received praise and acclamation, while inside feeling an unwilling resent-ment that I knew even at the time took away any pretension that I was "meriting" anything.

The passions, the perversities of the will, the innermost secret desires of the heart, keep thwarting the best moral intentions. Moralists are often tempted to mask their failures with dishonesty or rationalization. This is why moralism is often accompanied by hypocrisy, a show of external righteousness that masks the true story of what is happening inside.

Another way of coping when our moral reach exceeds our grasp is to push virtue out to the periphery of our experience—becoming a matter of voting right or holding the correct social positions or supporting virtuous causes—even while our personal or family lives become a wreck. We define down moral perfection, making it something easier and within our control. In doing so, of course, we generally end up violating the moral obligations that really count, those that have to do with our own behavior and our relationships to those around us.

Another problem inherent to moralism is that righteousness has a way of twisting itself into self-righteousness, a feeling of pride and superiority that undoes the virtue that is achieved. The problem is not only that people of the highest morals slip up. It seems that the very effort to be moralistic tends to breed harshness, pride, and even cruelty, hardly signs of being "a good person."

Certainly, "being good" is a laudable goal. The problem, if we are honest, is that no one seems able fully to achieve that goal. We don't really have the willpower, or the inner motivation, or the inner purity to achieve moral perfection.

Another approach to the spiritual life, besides moralism, is speculation, the assumption that knowledge is the key to spiritual fulfillment. If we only knew the truth, if we could only find the key to understanding the complexities of life, if only we attained the right knowledge, then we would be content. Thus we have the elaborate systems of metaphysics, the ingenious paradigms of explanation, the impulse to figure out the why of life.

Certainly, the pursuit of knowledge, like the pursuit of morality, is among the worthiest of human endeavors. And yet, as a spiritual path, it too keeps running into dead ends. The human mind is just not big enough to take in the whole of existence.

Many answers have been offered, but they keep changing, as the history of human thought shows. One school of philosophy is succeeded by another, and even scientific theories keep having to be revised. It seems impossible to settle upon truths that are final and indisputable.

Certainly spiritual truths—such as knowledge of an utterly transcendent and infinite God—stagger the human intellect. To paraphrase the Samaritan woman, the well is deep and we have nothing to draw with (John 4:11).

Furthermore, human systems have a way of reflecting human desires more than objective reality. Ideologies that claim to account for everything have often become the pretext for power plays, deception, and oppression. The Enlightenment of the French Revolution gave us the Reign of Terror and Napoleon. The liberal-sounding tenets of Marxism gave us the gulags. As with moralism, the way of speculation often becomes simply another occasion for human pride, manifesting itself in an elitism that scorns ordinary people or a private arrogance that shuts out the rest of the world. In the meantime, the truth seems ever more elusive, just beyond reach.

And even if we knew, what would we have? In Marlowe's *Dr. Faustus*, the hero sells his soul to the devil for knowledge. But when he finally knows for sure what he had dreamed of learning—the details of celestial mechanics, the disputed facts of astronomy, the heights and depths of the educated mind—the knowledge he has at great cost achieved suddenly seems pointless, unsatisfying, and unconnected to his true spiritual condition.

In my own case, I pored over books of every kind in my search for spiritual illumination. To be sure, they all contradicted each other, and I wondered about putting my trust in a single human being, no matter how wise he seemed, who knew as little as I did. But I was engaged with filling my head while neglecting my actual life.

Though the ways of moralism and speculation are followed by religious and non-religious people alike, perhaps the most appealing mode of spirituality today is mysticism: attaining the ecstatic experience of becoming one with God. Transcending ordinary life to attain direct communion with the divine, leaving behind this world to ascend into the spiritual realms, having a direct experience of the supernatural and tapping into its power for our own purposes—these have been the goals of mystics and spiritual masters of all religions. The techniques of achieving such experiences are varied, from ascetic self-denial to elaborate methodologies of meditation, but they all promise spiritual ecstasy and supernatural empowerment.

One problem here is the fine line between the self "becoming one with God" and the self becoming God. Merging with the divine can have as its hidden agenda self-deification. The most mystical religions, such as Hinduism, and the popular secularized mysticisms, such as those that constitute the New Age Movement, conclude by invoking "the god within." The climax of Hinduism is the realization that "Atman [the god of the inmost self] and Brahma [the transcendent deity] are one." New Age self-help seminars try to get across the idea that "you create your own reality." The ultimate discovery in many of these mystical systems, expressed more or less directly, is that "*you* are God."

Even Christian mystical experience, while drawing away from such formulations, can veer close to claiming supernatural power, from divine inspiration, with the Holy Spirit speaking to the person directly, to the power to work miracles. Mysticism can come dangerously close to the Serpent's primal temptation: "You will be like God" (Genesis 3:5).

Even when mysticism does not go that far, its temptation is to use God for one's own purposes—to achieve an intensely pleasurable experience, to score a "spiritual high," to gain power to make one's life more pleasant. This is the way of magicians and conmen, as well as spiritual masters. The notion itself that the spirit is something that can be "mastered" shows the limitations of mysticism. Even at its best, mysticism tends to retreat into the self, into the interior emotions, shutting out the exterior world and those who dwell therein. At least this was the way it was with me.

All three of these conventional approaches to spirituality involve human beings' expending strenuous effort to reach God, who is, by implication, an impassive observer, far above the fray, a goal that must be attained, a treasure that must be sought, discovered, and earned. Koeberle says that the three approaches to spirituality are tied to the various faculties of the human mind: moralism exerts the efforts of the will; speculation exerts the efforts of the intellect; mysticism exerts the efforts of the emotions.

Lutheran spirituality begins with the insight that *all* human effort to reach God is futile. The will, to use Luther's term, is in bondage—not only can we not fulfill the moral law perfectly, on the deepest level, we do not *want to*. The intellect is in a bondage of its own, bound by its limits and tainted by the sinful will. The emotions are likewise in bondage, apt more to lead us astray than to lead us to God. Far from ascending to God, we spend most of our time trying to run away from Him.

But God is no passive force. God is the one who is active, not human beings. The issue is not our ascent to God, but God's descent to us.

Lutheran spirituality is all about what God does. To rescue us from our miserable and depraved human condition, He became a human being Himself. The God-man Jesus Christ accomplished the perfection moralists only aspire to and took upon Himself the punishment for everyone's moral failures by dying on the cross. The spiritual life has to do with recognizing God's work—what He accomplished on the cross and what He continues to accomplish in people's lives through the Holy Spirit.

To use Koeberle's terms, Lutheran spirituality addresses the moral impulse of the will by the Law and Gospel. In place of speculation, the need of the intellect for knowledge is met by the Word of God. In place of a mystical union with God experienced by the emotions, Lutherans focus on God's union with human beings in Christ and the phenomenon of faith. In every case, God does it all.

LAW AND GOSPEL

When we stop speculating and look to what God Himself has to say in His Word, we find that our condition is more serious than we might have thought. The Bible indeed requires moral perfection. It holds up sublime moral truths and explores God's radical hatred of every kind of wrongdoing. Not only does it demand perfection, it goes on to intensify what that perfection entails. Not only external actions but internal feelings and motives must be absolutely pure. Jesus on the Sermon on the Mount condemns not only adultery but lust, not only murder but anger—promising the same judgment for both (Matthew 5:21–30).

The Law of God as unfolded in Scripture must make the most upright moralist squirm. With sufficient willpower, we might control our behavior, though that is difficult enough to do consistently. But how can we control what is happening inside us—the anger, lusts, and self-regard that threaten, if what the Bible says is true—to undo the merit of all our good deeds? Such feelings are not even matters of the will; they arise even against our wills, seemingly out of our control.

The Bible demands that we be righteous, but then tells us that "all our righteous acts are like filthy rags" (Isaiah 64:6). We learn that we are fallen, complicit in the disobedience and the curse of Adam and Eve (Genesis 3). In the New Testament, a single verse demolishes each brand of human spirituality: "There is no one righteous, not even one [so much for *moralism*!]; there is no one who understands [so much for *speculation*!]; no one who seeks God [so much for *mysticism*!]" (Romans 3:12).

A genuine confrontation with God's Law destroys complacency, security, and every shred of self-righteousness. Guilt rises up
in the gorge, and fear at the horrible prospect of eternal punishment, the fires of hell reserved for those who disobey the awful
righteousness of God. To be sure, one response would be to deny
it all, to insist that I really am a good person, that there is nothing wrong with my vices, and that God's Word isn't true at all.
But the Bible speaks with an authority that is difficult to evade,
and in one's heart of hearts God's Law rings true. Admitting one's
failure—and agreeing with one's condemnation—is the first step
of Lutheran spirituality.

For Lutherans, God's Law has many "uses"—to restrain evil in
society and to serve as a guide for the Christian life, ideas that
will be discussed in later chapters—but its "spiritual use" is to cut
through our layers of self-deception so that we realize just how
lost we really are. In biblical language, the Law brings with it the
"conviction of sin," inspiring "repentance."

The language of spirituality is so often the language of ecstasy,
of power, of supernal bliss, that the spiritual use of the law may
well seem negative, depressing, unpleasant, and indeed it is. Especially today, when guilt is treated like a pathology, and self-esteem
is considered the definition of psychological health, the notion
that spirituality begins with such a negative, self-effacing, even
despairing experience seems strange indeed.

But the Law is the prelude to the Gospel. Those broken by the
Law are convinced of their need and of their inability to save
themselves. Then the message that God does it all comes as an
astounding relief, as good news. Those who despair of achieving
perfection by themselves can hear the message of the cross—that
they can find totally free forgiveness through the work of Jesus
Christ—and cling to it, desperately, with every fiber of their being.
Then they become open to God's life-changing gifts.

When they do so, they are justified by faith. Christ's righteousness is counted as their own. The Law's demands for moral perfection are thus satisfied, vicariously but effectively. Christ's death counts for any punishment they deserve. They are utterly forgiven, released from fear, filled with gratitude for the sheer grace of God. Their illumination comes not from their own speculation, but from an encounter with the Word of God. They are connected to Christ, not in a mere mystical sense, as if they ascended into the spiritual realm, but actually, as the Holy Spirit descends into their lives. They are now in Christ, who said, "I am the way [so much for *moralism*], the truth [so much for *speculation*], and the life [so much for *mysticism*]" (John 14:6). As a result, through Christ, the will, the intellect, and the spirit are all set free.

Faith is not mere intellectual assent to certain beliefs. This would be the way of speculation. Nor is it any version of "positive thinking" or cosmic optimism, nor is it, as Kierkegaard describes it, a leap into what cannot be known. Faith is not an experience. This would be the way of mysticism.

Faith for Lutherans is certainly not a "decision to accept Christ," as it is described by later evangelicals. Making salvation a function of the will would be moralism, making salvation contingent, once again, upon what the human being does, a function of human effort, willpower, and action, in all of their actual futility.

Faith itself is considered by Lutherans to be a gift of God, created in the human heart as His action through the Holy Spirit. Faith has to do with trust, with conscious dependence on Christ, the assurance that, in fact, He will do it all. "For faith does not justify or save because it is a good work in itself," explains Melanchthon, "but only because it accepts the promised mercy."[2]

Properly speaking, it is Christ on the cross who saves. Faith is simply dependence on that sacrifice.

Much of Lutheranism, of course, accords with other Christian theologies. Other evangelicals emphasize the experience of conversion. Lutherans too believe in conversion. But the Law and the Gospel, the dynamics of repentance and the acceptance of Christ, are part of the fabric of Lutheran *spirituality*, not just a one-time occurrence but a pattern entered into again and again throughout one's life.

The pattern of conversion is repeated every Sunday, in the confession and absolution, in the pastor's sermon which is always a proclamation of Law and Gospel. Luther went even further. He said that we should be broken by the Law and animated by the Gospel *every day*: "The old Adam in us, together with all sins and evil lusts, should be drowned by daily sorrow and repentance and be put to death," he says in the catechism, explaining the significance of baptism; whereupon "the new man should come forth daily and rise up, cleansed and righteous, to live forever in God's presence."[3]

Those who have been justified by Christ are changed from the inside. Good works flow unconsciously from the work of Christ. Christians, however, have a double nature: their new spiritual nature from the indwelling Christ (Luther's "new man") and the old sinful nature from Adam ("the old Adam"). These are in constant conflict, so that the Christian's life is often one not of peace but of turmoil. Christians continually must fight temptation and will, despite all their efforts, fall into sin. But Christ is also at work in the Christian's life. The disciplines of prayer, confession, and the ministry of Word and Sacrament enable the Christian to grow in holiness and good works—a process known as sanctification.

There are times when the Christian particularly needs to hear the Law, and there are times when the Christian needs to hear the Gospel. Lutheran pastors, in their spiritual care of their parishioners, study how to distinguish and properly apply the Law and the Gospel. People who exhibit pride, willful sin, and self-righteousness need to hear the Law—otherwise, they will be oblivious to their need for Christ. Those, however, who are hurting, who are plagued by guilt, hopelessness, and despair, need to hear the Gospel.

Thus, Lutheran spirituality, properly speaking, is not some static state of bliss, but a dynamic oscillation between lows and highs, knowledge of sin and knowledge of forgiveness, repentance and assurance. The Gospel is to predominate, however, in the words of C. F. W. Walther, so that the Lutheran Christian lives in a state of grace.[4]

THE PARADOXES OF LUTHERANISM

Thus, Lutherans tend to be highly conscious of sin, without falling into moralism. They treasure theology and have a rich intellectual tradition, while emphasizing the limits of speculative reason and stressing their utter dependence on the revelation of God's Word. They are skeptical of mystical emotionalism, but they cultivate an intense inner piety and a worship centered in ineffable mysteries. As will be seen, the central paradox of Christianity, the incarnation, that Christ is both fully God and fully man, is echoed in the "both/and's" that resonate throughout Lutheranism, from its sacramental theology to the role of the Christian in the secular world.

In its theology and in its spirituality, Lutheranism is a system of paradoxes, of apparent contradictions that are actually two poles of truth and experience. The Christian, according to Luther, is *simul justus et peccator*, at the same time righteous and a sinner. The Christian is totally free, yet a slave—in Christian service—to everyone. Such paradoxes are not just formulas of doctrine, but, as will be seen, polarities that comprehend the complexities of the spiritual life.

When I discovered the radical depths of the Gospel, I found the impulses that variously made me a moralist, a speculator, and a mystic all resolved—or rather put in tension with each other and swallowed up in the cross.

NOTES

[1] Adolf Koeberle, *The Quest for Holiness*, trans. John C. Mattes (New York: Harper & Brothers, 1936; rpt. Evansville, IN: Ballast Press, 1995), 2.

[2] "Apology of the Augsburg Confession," Article IV, line 56, in *The Book of Concord: The Confessions of the Evangelical Lutheran Church*, trans. Theodore G. Tappert (Philadelphia: Fortress Press, 1959), 114.

[3] "The Small Catechism of Dr. Martin Luther," Article IV, question 4, in *The Book of Concord*, 349.

[4] For the classic treatment of Law and Gospel, see C. F. W. Walther, *On the Proper Distinction Between Law and Gospel* (St. Louis: Concordia Publishing House, 1986).

tHe meaNs of gRace

THE PRESENCE OF GOD

When a Lutheran is asked "When were you saved?" the answer is often something on the order of "about two thousand years ago, when Jesus died on the cross and then rose from the dead." Christianity has to do not so much with a code of behavior or a system of belief or a set of experiences but with Christ.[1] We are saved solely by the action of God: He is the one who saved us by performing everything we could not.

God caused Himself to be born as a human being. Jesus Christ, God in the flesh, kept the moral Law perfectly. And then, when He was being tortured to death on the cross, in perhaps the profoundest miracle imaginable, He took upon Himself every sin, every transgression ever committed, and suffered every punishment we deserve. Jesus died because the wages of sin is death (Romans 6:23). More than that, when He cried out in his death agony, "My God, my God, why have you forsaken me?" (Matthew 27:46), Jesus was experiencing the Holy God turning away from all the evil in the world—which Jesus was bearing in His body—the same withdrawal of God that constitutes hell. But then, having atoned for the sins of the world, Jesus rose again.

According to the terms of this mysterious exchange, all of the sin that the Christian has ever done—all of the selfishness, the hate, the secret vices, the greedy egotism that breaks out in hurting others—all of this is credited to Jesus. And killed on the cross. Conversely, Christ's righteousness—all of the goodness He showed in healing the sick, feeling compassion for the multitudes, resisting temptation, driving the moneychangers out of the Temple—is credited to the Christian. And since Jesus rose from the dead to a new life, the Christian does too.

This means that the Christian has the same favor with God, the same access, the same assurance of eternal life, as Jesus does. When we come before the Holy God, He does not turn away in judgment; rather, He sees us through the lens of Christ—we might even say, He sees us *as* Christ. Our mediator claims all of our sins and has paid for them with His blood. He provides all of the good works we need, clothing us in His—not our—righteousness. This is what it means to be saved.

Lutheran theologians speak of "objective justification." Strictly speaking, justification took place outside of ourselves, in the actual historical events of Christ's death and resurrection. On the cross, two millenia ago, our salvation was accomplished as an objective event. And yet, the objectivity of what happened on the cross has a profound spiritual implication for us now. Our own miserable little vices and perversities were *there*—right on the cross with Jesus. Those things that we feel so guilty for, Jesus objectively bore in His body; thus, despite any subjective feelings we may have of guilt over what we have done, forgiveness is also objective.

This is an astonishing teaching, of course. It may seem hard to believe when parsed logically or morally or theologically. It may seem too easy, too good to be true. It is precisely "the good news," the "Gospel" or, in Greek, the *evangel* from which the first evangelicals took their name and established every facet of their spirituality.

Other Christians, including others who call themselves evangelicals, consider that they were saved when they "made a decision for Christ" or were converted or experienced an encounter with the Holy Spirit or the like. Lutheran evangelicals, while certainly believing in conversion, do not talk that way. Looking at salvation in terms of decisions and experiences shifts the focus away from what Christ has done to what I have done. We are back to the unevangelical dilemma of having to save ourselves—by what we decide or what we experience or what we do. This lands us back into moralism and its accompanying failures and uncertainties and self-deceptions. Instead of building our hope on the shifting sands of our own works or inner lives, we can have the confidence that what Christ did for us is a fact. Lutherans are thus always wrenching their attention from themselves to remember the concrete objectivity of what God has done for them in Christ.

But what is the connection between our lives, here and now, and what happened on Golgotha, the hill on which Jesus was crucified? Though Christ atoned for the sins of the entire world, it is clear that not everyone has faith. If there is an objective justification, there must be a subjective justification, wherein the fact of Christ's work on the cross has its impact in the life of an individual human being. If faith is not a decision nor an experience nor some inner work, and if salvation is totally the work of God, it would seem that faith too must be the work of God.

So how do we attain a saving, life-changing faith?

The answer, in Lutheran spirituality, has to do with the so-called *means of grace*. We are connected to Christ, and the Holy Spirit works both faith and good works in our lives by means of the Word and the Sacraments.

THE WORD OF GOD

Central to every level of Lutheran theology and spirituality—its source, its method, and its practice— is the insight that God Himself addresses human beings through human language. Other religions look for "visions" of God; other theologies expect God to manifest Himself through a particular experience. Some Christians assume the Holy Spirit communicates to them directly, as an inner impulse or a personal revelation. For Lutherans, God comes from the outside; the Holy Spirit is to be found objectively. God speaks directly and effectually to us in His Word.

All human beings, of every culture, have language, which is the means by which individuals can form relationships with each other. Language enables individuals to communicate themselves with others, to form relationships, from friendships to families to societies. Language makes thought possible, opening up the possibility of ideas, the accumulation of knowledge, the creation of arts and inventions. Scholars are just now discovering the depths upon depths of human language, how it is innate to the mind, how it shapes cultures, how it, in effect, defines what is human. Many scientists are going further, finding that language seems to be built into existence itself. The genetic codes of DNA, the structures of chemistry, and the laws of physics seem to be analagous to the grammatical structures of language.

No wonder, since God created the whole universe by His Word (Psalm 33:6; John 1:1–3). God is no abstract force, as in many religions, but a Person. As such, He thinks, loves, and expresses Himself, so that He has language. He created human beings in His image, as persons, and so we too have language. The fall marred the gift of language, sin tainting language so that it degenerated into confusion and misunderstanding as we see in the Tower of Babel (Genesis 11); but the Holy Spirit at Pentecost enabled people to understand, once again, each other's tongues (Acts 2).

On the simplest level, it is language—of some kind, including the signs of the deaf— that makes possible all relationships. We must communicate or we feel alone. Language enables us to share what we are thinking and feeling—our very selves—with someone else. Friends and lovers must talk to each other. The lack of communication wrecks marriages, not to mention businesses and governments.

Why shouldn't God also communicate and establish relationships by means of language? Not by vague intimations or mystical intuitions, but real language, with words and grammar and meanings—language that is accessible to everyone, that can be written down. The Christian's relationship to God, like all other relationships, thrives on two-way conversations—the Christian speaks to God by prayer, and God speaks to the Christian who reads His Word.

Critics of Lutheranism say that, well, the Bible is a human document, written over centuries by many different human authors working in specific cultural and historical contexts. Moreover, though the gospels of Christ's life and the epistles of the apostles date from the very beginnings of the church, the complete canon of Scripture was not even established until the fourth century. Surely, then, the church—which decided which books would be included in Scripture—is prior to the Word.

Lutherans insist that the Bible, though written by human beings, is indeed the Word of God. But the Word of God is not the

Bible alone. The Son of God, the Second Person of the Trinity, is described in that Bible as the Word of God, so that Jesus is "the Word made flesh" (John 1:1–3, 14). What the pastor preaches is the Word of God. Every proclamation of the Gospel, whether in a sermon or in a layperson's informal witnessing to a friend, is a dissemination of God's Word. This oral word, insofar as it is the message of the Bible, is God's Word delivered by a human voice.

It is a Lutheran truism that God generally works through means. Just as God is not ashamed to inspire the utterances of fallen human beings, to have His truths written in human language with paper and ink, He is not ashamed to have His Word communicated by the halting speech of His followers. The main difference between God's Word and merely human words, is that God—the Holy Spirit—promises to be at work whenever His Word is spoken. "My word that goes out from my mouth," says the Lord, "will not return to me empty, but will accomplish what I desire and achieve the purpose for which I sent it" (Isaiah 55:11).

To return to the objections, the Word is, in fact, prior to the church. Even before the Bible was completely written, no one could know about Jesus—and thus join the church—unless they heard about Him. The words used to explain who Jesus was, what He did, and the forgiveness He offers, were the Word of God. The early evangelists were proclaiming the Gospel (God's Word), a message which could be traced back to the teachings of the first apostles (who taught God's Word), who heard it from Jesus Himself (God's Word made flesh). The apostolic testimony was written down from the beginning, along with the more ancient prophetic writings of the Old Testament, and later the various books were collected and printed together, but it was always the Word that God was using to bring people to Himself.

"How can they believe in the one of whom they have not heard? And how can they hear without someone preaching to them?" asks St. Paul. "Consequently, faith comes from hearing the message, and the message is heard through the word of Christ" (Romans 10:14, 17). And that Word, whether oral or written, enfleshed in Jesus or preached from a modern-day pulpit, is powerful, incisive, and convicting: "For the Word of God is living and active. Sharper than any double-edged sword, it penetrates even to dividing soul and spirit, joints and marrow; it judges the thoughts and attitudes of the heart" (Hebrews 4:12).

THE BIBLE

"No prophecy of Scripture came about by the prophet's own interpretation," says the Bible about itself. "For prophecy never had its origin in the will of man, but men spoke from God as they were carried along by the Holy Spirit" (2 Peter 1:20–21). God, in His direct inspiration and providential control of history, caused His Word to be put into writing. Consequently, Christians believe that "all Scripture is God-breathed" (1 Timothy 3:16).

That God's Word is written in a Book, which anyone can read whenever they want, sounds unspiritual to many people. They prefer communication with the divine to be more vague and esoteric, channeled, perhaps, by some oracle, or encoded in some sort of secret riddle, or relegated to the realm of mystical experience. But Christians believe that God's Word is something tangible, written down in ink and paper, accessible and objective.

The Scriptures are true. "My neighbor and I—in short, all men—may err and deceive," writes Luther in his *Large Catechism*, "but God's Word cannot err."[1] Not only is it true, it is truth. As Jesus Himself says, "Your word is truth" (John 17:17).

Human reason can figure out quite a lot of truth. The great medieval theologian Thomas Aquinas believed that reason can even prove that there is a God (though other Christians disagree).

But reason, Aquinas went on to say, cannot tell us very much about that God—what He is like, His purposes, His disposition towards human beings. For that, for knowledge of the utterly transcendent, we need Him to reveal Himself. We need God to tell us about Himself, His works in history, His will, and what He has done to rescue us. And how can we know these things apart from their expression in human language? We are, again, utterly dependent on His Word.

Lutherans and other Christians agree, then, that the Bible is authoritative. It is the source and test, the touchstone, of all valid theology. Though God's Word exists whenever human beings proclaim Christ, what humans say cannot be considered God's Word unless it agrees with and is an exposition of what the Bible says.

Lutherans and other Christians agree that the Bible gives us accurate information about God's actions in history. We would never know about the incarnation or that the atonement happened, if we could not read about them. Otherwise, these objective, historical events would dissolve into time, and we would be oblivious to them. The narratives and teachings of the Bible tell us what we need to know.

Lutherans, however, see something else happening when we read or hear the Bible. It is a means of grace. The words of the Bible do not merely convey information, they convey the Holy Spirit. "The Word of God is living and active." The words of Scripture actually connect us to what they are describing. As we read those words on the page, God is literally and objectively present and working, inscribing in our hearts the gift of faith.

Many Christians, including many Protestants committed to scriptural authority, balk at this exceedingly high view of the Bible held by Lutherans. True, the Bible tells us historical and theological truths, but surely God is not present in paper and ink. One ought not worship a book. Lutherans are charged with committing "bibliolatry." And yet, Lutherans insist that the Holy Spirit is indeed present and at work in the words of Scripture. They deny that they are worshiping a book, as such, but they see the Bible as a means of grace, as sacramental.

The content of God's Word is Law and Gospel. The Bible reveals God's holiness, His will, His demands, and His judgments. Reading them can be a devastating experience. The Bible also reveals His love, His grace, and His promises—how God constantly rescued His children from their sin-caused slavery, how Christ offered Himself as the expiation for our sins.

The point of Bible reading is not merely to learn about God, to see how we should behave, or to gain principles for successful living, though the Bible does communicate such things. To read the Bible as a spiritual venture is to be confronted, in the most personal terms, with God Himself. This confrontation is terrifying: An honest reading of God's absolute requirements, His furious judgment against the smallest infraction, can only fill the reader with guilt, panic, and despair. This confrontation is also healing— the reader comes to realize that this God of wrath is also the God of grace, that from the beginning He provided for sacrificial blood to cover His people's sins, that He came in Jesus, that His wrath is swallowed up in the cross. As we read the history and precepts, the poetry and the narratives and the apostolic letters, we encounter the Law and the Gospel, through which the Spirit works to change our hearts and bind us to Christ.

I remember when I first began to read the Bible seriously. As I read the Old Testament, I was overcome with its sublimity, later horrified by passages such as God's commands that the Canaanites be slaughtered. I began to realize that God was something "other," someone far above my comprehension. I realized that I had been constructing God according to my preferences, positing qualities that I liked and ascribing them to the deity I believed in. In effect,

I was making God in my image. But the God I was reading about in the Bible, whose energy blasted those who touched the Ark of the Covenant without the mediation of blood, was very different from myself, numinous, holy, and dangerous. And yet He rang true.

I probably never really believed in the vague, domesticated spirit of niceness that I had constructed for myself and found in my humane liberal theology. The real universe, with its danger and consequences and hard edges, such as cancer, shows no trace of having been created by such a sentimental deity. I probably knew, deep down inside, that I was making up a private little religion to make myself feel better, and that atheism made far better sense. But this God I was reading about in the Bible had hard edges. He is absolute, utterly mysterious, and despite all appearances radically righteous. I began to see God in a completely different light, the light of holiness. And I saw myself in the rebellious children of Israel, ungrateful, inconsistent, and idolatrous.

And yet, I saw while I was reading that when God's children were nearly absorbed—and enslaved—by the pagan cultures they wanted to emulate, God kept sending them deliverers: Moses, the judges, the prophets, and the good kings. He also gave them the temple and curious rites in which their sins could be covered by blood. By the time I got to the New Testament, reading the life of Christ, it all came together, and the epistles of St. Paul made the fact of my salvation vividly clear.

I did not know the terminology at the time, much less the theology; but what I was experiencing in reading the Bible was the Law, which was convicting me of my sinfulness and awakening in me the knowledge of my lost condition, and the Gospel, which assured me of my forgiveness in Christ. Much later, when I became a Lutheran, I understood the sense in which the Word of God,

working through Law and Gospel, is the means by which the Holy
Spirit bestows the gift of faith.

THE SACRAMENTS: BAPTISM

Today is an age of both unbelief and hyperspirituality. Religion is fine, as long as it is safely interior, as long as it is vague and
immaterial. It may seem unspiritual to assert that a physical book,
ink printed on paper, can have such effects, or that the Word of
God preached from a pulpit—which is nothing, after all, but
sound waves vibrating in the air, striking the tympanum of the
ear and processed by the physical brain—should be the means by
which the Holy Spirit creates faith and saves souls.

The Word of God itself speaks of other tangible means of grace,
which, by the power of that same Word, also convey Christ and
create faith. These are the sacraments: Baptism and Holy Communion. Lutheran spirituality is a sacramental spirituality, centered in the conviction that the Holy Spirit actually descends in
the waters of Baptism, and that Christ is really present in the bread
and wine of Holy Communion.

It is certainly very odd that water, bread, and wine should have
such significance—though perhaps it is no more odd than that ink
on paper and sound waves should convey the Word of the infinite God—an unlikelihood that will be taken up in the next chapter. But Lutherans believe that the Gospel is conveyed, objectively, when a human being, even an infant, is baptized. The
Gospel is also conveyed, objectively, when the Lord's Supper is
reenacted and the communicant is fed with bread and wine, in
which is present the actual body and blood of Jesus Christ given
for the forgiveness of sins. These, again, are astounding claims; but
they are more examples of the objectivity of God's grace and the

fact that God accomplishes everything for our salvation, and that all we need to do is to receive His gifts.

Just as God was present in His temple with the children of Israel, sustaining them with worship and sacrifices, so He is present today in His church. The Word of God not only justifies sinners individually, but also calls them together into the body of the church. The Holy Spirit is strongly at work in local congregations, unlikely as it may sometimes seem, as the pastor proclaims the Word and teaches and applies it to his people. That Word is also operative in the life of the church, in a particularly personal and intimate way, when the pastor baptizes and when he feeds his flock with the Lord's Supper.

"Baptism ... now saves you," says the Bible. "Not the removal of dirt from the body but the pledge of a good conscience toward God. It saves you by the resurrection of Jesus Christ" (1 Peter 3:21). Such words are clear and can hardly be explained away. Baptism does save, not as a merely physical washing, but because it connects us to the resurrection of Christ. Baptism does something. St. Paul could hardly be more explicit:

> Don't you know that all of us who were baptized
> into Christ Jesus were baptized into his death? We were
> therefore buried with him through baptism into death in
> order that, just as Christ was raised from the dead
> through the glory of the Father, we too may live a new
> life. If we have been united with him like this in his death,
> we will certainly also be united with him in his resurrec-
> tion (Romans 6: 3–5).

According to this Scripture, Baptism unites a person to Christ, specifically, to His death and resurrection. In Baptism we are immersed in His death. When we are baptized, we are "buried with him." When we are baptized, we are "united with him in his resurrection."

These are strong words. Lutherans, who are taught to cling to God's Word rather than to try to interpret it away, simply take them literally. To be baptized is to die—with Christ—and rise again. It is the link between now, this time and place, and Golgotha and the empty tomb. Someone who has been baptized can have the assurance that he or she has a share in Christ's death and resurrection. Someone who has been baptized has been born again.

I know that to say this will scandalize many evangelicals. Christians of all traditions can learn much from Lutheranism, but it is in its sacramentalism that they have to draw the line. Again, it is not my purpose in this book to argue for this doctrine or explain it in its depths—consult the sources listed "for further reading" for that. But the Lutheran understanding of Baptism is, in fact, the most evangelical of doctrines.

Certainly, Lutherans believe in conversion, in the necessity of a personal faith. They also reject the rather magical view of Baptism, the view that it saves by virtue of the act itself. "How can water do such great things?" is the obvious question in Luther's Small Catechism. "It is not the water indeed that does them, but the word of God which is in and with the water, and faith, which trusts such word of God in the water."[2] Nor is Baptism a human work, some ceremony which placates the divine; Baptism—like every other saving act—is the work of God. As Luther explains in the Large Catechism, "To be baptized in God's name is to be baptized not by men but by God himself. Although it is performed by men's hands, it is nevertheless truly God's own act."[3]

Consider, for example, the Baptism of infants. A mere baby cannot understand the meaning of this ritual. A baby has no knowledge of the Bible, no moral formation, no will capable of making a commitment to Christ. How can Lutherans say that a baptized baby is a Christian, that the child has been born again, no less? And how can they square their teaching on baptismal regeneration with their teaching on justification by faith?

Infant Baptism, in fact, is perhaps the best illustration of justification by faith. A distinctive Lutheran teaching about Baptism is that baptized infants do, in fact, have faith. To be sure, a baby does not have much knowledge or capacity for choice—but faith is not a matter of intellectual mastery, nor is it a decision. Faith is trust, a relationship of utter dependence on Christ. Does a baby, in all of its incapacity, trust its mother and father? Does it have a relationship of utter dependence with its parents? Isn't the love of the mother for her child something the baby knows, constituting the most heartfelt reality of its little existence? If a baby can have faith in its parents—resting securely dependent in their love and care—why can't the baby have faith in its heavenly Father?

In justification, the human being is purely passive, purely receptive. Salvation, again, is not by works, not by moral effort or by acquiring knowledge or by cultivating a mystical experience. Salvation is simply receiving a free gift from God. A baby receiving Baptism models that passive reception, which adults constantly struggle against in their zeal to save themselves by their own efforts. This is why when Jesus Himself was describing faith, conversion, and the Christian life, He offered a little child as the model:

He called a little child and had him stand among them. And he said:

> I tell you the truth, unless you change and become like little children, you will never enter the kingdom of heaven. Therefore, whoever humbles himself like this child is the greatest in the kingdom of heaven (Matthew 18:2–4).

A helpless child becomes our role model for conversion ("unless you change"). In justification, there is no room for human pride at all, either in one's capacities or in one's works ("whoever humbles himself like this child"). In Baptism, an infant passively receives God's grace, is united to Christ, and is changed. The Holy Spirit dwells in the child, who subsequently has a living faith, which must be continually nourished by hearing God's Word, just as a baby, once born, must still be fed or it will die.

But we must not sentimentalize Baptism. It is not a mere naming ceremony. For all the good feelings enjoyed by the parents, relatives, friends, and the congregation, for all the cuteness of the baby in its little lacy robe, in Baptism the child sacramentally dies. The waters of Baptism signify a drowning, as well as a cleansing. Baptism is, as the New Testament says, a burial.

In Baptism, the child is also named. But joined to the child's unique, personal name is the name of God. In fact, what makes a Baptism is not just the water, but the name of God ("I baptize you in the name of the Father, Son, and Holy Spirit"). This Word of God invokes His presence, and in the sacrament the child's identity is taken "in" to the identity of the Father, who created the child, the Son, who redeemed her, and the Holy Spirit, who leads her into faith.

Baptism plays a continual role in the spiritual life of Lutherans. We are always told to "remember your Baptism." Every day when you wash your face, said Luther, you should think of your Baptism. What he described in the catechism about Baptism applies every day of the Christian's life. To quote again, "The old Adam in us, together with all sins and evil lusts, should be drowned by daily sorrow and repentance and be put to death," so that "the new man should come forth daily and rise up, cleansed and righteous, to live forever in God's presence."[4]

The fact of one's baptism is also tied to the assurance of salvation. Many Christians today worry about whether they *really* made a personal decision for Jesus Christ and accepted Him as their Lord and Savior. In fact, it has become a fixture of large evangelical rallies to invite people to make a decision and come forward, just in case they really hadn't before. The altar call has become something of an evangelical sacrament. (I once had a student who wrote a story about a man who *almost* went forward—and probably would have if the preacher would have had the congregation sing one more chorus of the invitation hymn—only to die in a car wreck that very night, sending his soul to perdition.) The emphasis, though, on the inner movement of the will—besides putting the focus on what the *person* does to be saved, rather than what Christ has done—is inherently subjective and thus uncertain. Another kind of uncertainty, inherent to others who believe in salvation by grace alone, is the fear of maybe not being among those to whom God has chosen to give the gift of faith. Luther answered those who agonized over the question of whether or not they were of God's elect by pointing to a fact outside themselves: "You are a baptized child of God," he would tell them. In times of doubt, fear, and even despair, to those who worried about God's love for them, to those who questioned their salvation and their participation in Christ, Christians should not look inward, where they will probably find even more reasons to doubt their salvation. Grace, Lutherans insist, is objective. Christians in need of assurance should understand that their salvation is an objective fact, sealed in an event in space and time, as tangible as water.

Though Lutherans are always being told "remember your Baptism," the meaning is usually "remember that you have been baptized," since the actual event usually escapes the memory. But I actually can remember my Baptism.

Everything that has been said here holds true when adults are baptized too. I was baptized as an adult—or rather, as an adolescent—so that I have the privilege of actually recalling what it was like to be baptized. This was long before I was a Lutheran.

(Lutherans, by the way, accept Baptism from any Christian church—after all, it is the Word and the Name of God that, with the water, constitutes the Baptism, not the theology of the pastor. Strictly speaking, it is not a work of human beings at all. As Luther said, it is God that is really doing the baptizing.)

At the time—I think I was around 12—I was probably as unknowing as an infant. I had gone up at the altar call (an un-Lutheran practice), and was baptized by total immersion (another un-Lutheran practice, though certainly acceptable and, I would say, rather effective in conveying the sense of drowning and getting buried).

I remember the experience vividly. The baptistry was a tank of water built into the wall of the sanctuary at the front of the church, normally hidden by a curtain; when there would be a Baptism, the curtains would be open, revealing a backdrop of trees, water, and sky, intending to represent the Jordan River. It always struck me as a solemn, mysterious event when those curtains were open and someone got baptized. Some of the other young people in my age group were getting baptized too. I remember when it was my turn to step down the concrete steps into the water, finding to my relief the water was warm. I was wearing old jeans and a t-shirt under a white robe, which billowed in the water. Baptizing me in the name of the Father, Son, and Holy Ghost, the pastor used the nickname everyone knew me by—I being a junior, which may be why I still think of myself as that name. I put my hands over my nose, as we had been instructed, and leaned back into the pastor's arms, the warm waters closing over me. I was down in the water for what seemed like a long time, and then brought to the surface in a rush. Gasping, and spluttering, and trying to catch my breath, I felt exultant.

After it was over, after I had gone back into a room and changed my clothes, still damp, I really did feel cleansed, born again. The next day, filled with zeal for the Lord, I went up to my best friend on the school yard and did my first "witnessing," wanting him to have that same rebirth that I had.

"Earl," I said, "you've really got to get baptized."

"Why?" he replied, not unreasonably.

I was strangely taken aback and, not being very well instructed, did not really know how to answer him. "Well," I said, "it's fun." But my heart sank as I gave such a pathetic testimony to my faith. I knew there was more to it than that and that I needed to know more. I was an infant after all.

Again, mine was not a Lutheran baptism, but even though it was later that I read C. S. Lewis, for my first real introduction to the ideas of Christianity, and though it was much later that I read and believed the Bible, and much, much later that I was received into the Lutheran church. This was still my beginning.

THE SACRAMENTS: HOLY COMMUNION

To recall the various patterns of Lutheran spirituality: In our relationship with God, He is the one who acts. We do not seek Him; He seeks us. (Notice how this is dramatized in Christ's parable of the lost sheep, Luke 15:4–7.) We do not love God; He loves us ("This is love: not that we loved God, but that he loved us and sent his Son as an atoning sacrifice for our sins" [1 John 4:10]). As in Francis Thompson's poem "The Hound of Heaven," we try to run away from God, but He pursues us, relentlessly tracking us down. Instead of our ascending to God, He descends to us. Though Christians are called to action in the world, as will be discussed in a later chapter, in our relationship with God, everything hinges on God's action.

This action is *objective*. God comes to us from the outside. Though it is true that Christ and the Holy Spirit come to dwell in our hearts, they are not a mere function of our psychological state, our experiences, or our inward selves. The rich spiritual literature of the Lutheran tradition always tells struggling or doubtful Christians not to look inward—to do so is to see only the sinful self—but to look to something objective and tangible: to the cross, to God's Word, to the immutable promises of God.

The confidence that those promises apply to me, that I am a Christian and have been saved, is established not by the vagaries of memories, decisions, or sensations of being elected or not, but by an objective, tangible historical event. "When our sins or conscience oppress us," Luther writes, "we must retort, 'But I am baptized! And if I am baptized, I have the promise that I shall be saved and have eternal life, both in soul and body.'"[5]

Furthermore, God acts through *material reality*. The very word "spiritual" is taken as the opposite of the "material," so that religion is assumed to be some sort of escape from the "material realm," its values opposed to every kind of "materialism." It is true that many religions, such as those of the East, have that quality— in Hinduism, the material world is seen as an illusion spun by a demon, and to be saved means to escape the bondage of the senses and the attachment to physical existence. Christianity, by contrast, has always affirmed the religious significance of the physical.

The first article of the Christian creed is the doctrine of creation, in which God not only created the material universe but saw that "it was very good" (Genesis 1:31). The second article is the doctrine of the incarnation, which likewise affirms the physical realm by teaching that God Himself "came down from heaven, was incarnate by the Holy Spirit of the virgin Mary, and was made man."[6] In Christ, "the Word became flesh" (John 1:14).

In the third article, we find that the Holy Spirit manifests Himself in earthly entities, from the "communion of saints" that is the church through the physical resurrection of the dead.

The means of grace—the Word and Sacraments—are likewise material things. Mundane acts such as going to church and (as we shall see) living in a family and going to work are charged with spiritual significance.

The means of grace through which the Holy Spirit works on us to create faith and spiritual growth are *evangelical*. That is, they bear the Gospel of forgiveness through Christ. They do not work as talismans to make the rains fall or our business successful (though we can pray for such things). Their purpose is to communicate *grace*, the unmerited favor of God that grants eternal life.

In the sacrament of Holy Communion, all of Lutheran spirituality is crystalized: God acts, objectively, through matter, embodying the Gospel and promising the forgiveness of sin. And, more than that—or rather, making all of these efficacious—is the *real presence* of Jesus Christ. This is another astonishing claim, one which many Christians draw back from, but one that is at the pulsing heart of Lutheran evangelicalism.

The Bible records that Jesus, hours before His arrest, broke bread and said, "This is my body given for you," and then took wine and said, "This is my blood of the covenant, which is poured out for many for the forgiveness of sins." He also told His followers to "do this in remembrance of me" (Matthew 26:26–28; Luke 22:19–20). Surely, the Bible must mean that the bread and wine *symbolize* the body and blood of Christ. No, Lutherans do not try to interpret or explain away or rationalize what the Word of God says.

There are certainly other passages that indicate that something extraordinary is going on in the Lord's Supper. St. Paul solemnly warns the Corinthians, "whoever eats the bread or drinks the cup of the Lord in an unworthy manner will be guilty of sinning against the body and blood of the Lord. A man ought to examine himself before he eats of the bread and drinks of the cup. For anyone who eats and drinks without recognizing the body of the Lord eats and drinks judgment on himself" (1 Corinthians 4:27–29). This doesn't sound merely symbolic. It sounds as if "the body and blood of the Lord" are *there*—that they are there in power, and that they must be recognized. At any rate, the Lutherans' exceedingly high view of the sacraments derives directly from their exceedingly high view of God's Word.

So—what if it is true? The *risen* Christ is actually present in the elements of bread and wine. We sometimes speak of searching for God, wishing we could have met Jesus, saying that we could believe if only Christ would appear to us: And here He is.

Not only is Christ present at the altar, He gives Himself to us. As we eat the bread, we are receiving, in an intimate and personal way, His body that was broken on the cross. When we sip the wine, we are receiving His blood that sealed the covenant, assuring the forgiveness of sin. We are literally united with Christ—Christ crucified, resurrected, and ascended—bridging the gap between here and Golgotha, now and eternity.

It has been said that this contact with Christ is more direct and closer and more intimate than what His disciples enjoyed. Again, Christ comes to us. It is not something we do, but something Christ does, which we have only to receive. The Lord's Supper is nothing less than the Gospel.

Perhaps the most significant of God's Words which constitute the sacrament, Luther points out, are "given for you."[7] The one who receives the bread and wine hears that Christ's body and blood, here offered, are "for you."

There is nothing vague here. There is no need to worry about my decisions, or whether or not I have been elected to be saved, or whether or not I am sinful. In the sacrament, Christ gives Himself to me. All of His promises and everything that He did for my redemption and forgiveness on the cross, are made so tangible I can taste them. I am touching, in fact, the risen Christ, as the first disciples did. And God's Word, ringing in my ears as I take this nourishment, tells me that His body and blood are for *me*. That means that my sins are actually forgiven, that I can be assured of God's favor.

When I first started going to a Lutheran church, I was mesmerized simply by watching the people go up for Communion and hearing what the pastor was saying to them. We couldn't go, of course, until we had been thoroughly instructed. We also had to become actual members of this particular community of believers, this "communion," so intimate is the fellowship established by this eating and drinking. So at first I just watched: Jesus giving His body and blood for that teenager, that mother of the baby, that doctor, that lady in the wheelchair, "for you," the pastor kept saying, "for you, for you."

Sometimes the parishioners shuffling up to the Communion rail and back may have been simply caught up in a routine—though at other times I would be startled by a seraphic expression on one of the faces—but the routine doesn't matter. God routinely feeds His people, with their daily bread and with Himself. It is His action, and even our blindness or dull insensibility does not take anything away from His gifts.

Though I too sometimes take for granted Holy Communion, there are other times when I am overwhelmed by Christ's real presence. When I had my first Communion, it was sort of like my Baptism. The wafer was light, but it had to be chewed. "This is the true body of your Lord and Savior Jesus Christ," I heard the pastor say. And the wine surprised me by its sharpness, the sour but sweet taste according with the words I was hearing: "This is the true blood of your Lord and Savior Jesus Christ." It was all so tangible, so real.

Without food, we would starve to death. We have to eat to fuel our physical life; otherwise, we grow weak and waste away. The only food that can sustain our bodies comes from the death of other living things. Whether we are nourishing ourselves from a bloody steak or ripped up plants in a vegetarian casserole, there can be no life, even on the physical level, apart from the sacrifice of other life. What is true for physical life is true for spiritual life— we can only live if there has been a sacrifice. And we can only live if we have continual nourishment.

The Gospel of Christ converts us, but it also nourishes us. We need to keep receiving Christ over and over again. In the sacramental spirituality of Lutheranism, the Word and Sacraments are means of grace. They are tangible, material means used by God to convey the Gospel of Christ, who converts us, feeds us, and is actually present in His Church.

NOTES

[1] "The Large Catechism of Dr. Martin Luther," in *The Book of Concord: The Confessions of the Evangelical Lutheran Church*, trans. Theodore G. Tappert (Philadelphia: Fortress Press, 1959), 444.

[2] *Dr. Luther's Small Catechism* (St. Louis: Concordia Publishing House, 1943), 17.

[3] "The Large Catechism," 437.

[4] "The Small Catechism of Dr. Martin Luther," Article IV, question 4, in *The Book of Concord*, 349.

[5] "The Large Catechism," 442.

[6] The Nicene Creed, in *The Book of Concord*, 18.

[7] See the Small Catechism and the Large Catechism in *The Book of Concord*, 352, 450.

the theology of the cross

THE HIDDENNESS OF GOD

It seems strange to think that Christ is actually present in such a saving way in that little styrofoam-like wafer of bread or in the small sip of astringent wine. Or that God speaks to us in a literal book of ink, paper, and binding. Or that the pastor's sermon is used by the Holy Spirit to create faith in our hearts. These are rather spectacular claims for what goes on in an ordinary church service, with its weakly sung hymns, babies crying in the background, and everyday people fidgeting in their pews. It's hardly credible to think that such a mundane and frequently dull setting could be the scene of such high and holy spiritual presences.

One might say the same thing, of course, about the central event in Christianity. God came down from heaven to live as an itinerant Jewish carpenter, who ends up getting executed by torture! One would think that He would come as a king, accepting the veneration of His people and conquering His enemies. That He came in weakness, humiliation, rejection, and suffering is, to say the least, unexpected.

People today who seek to be spiritual must confess that God sometimes seems far away. The ordinariness of everyday life, the material burdens that one must live through, the routines, and the practical preoccupations of life often smother any sense of transcendence. And then there is the fact of actual suffering. When we face failure or disease or loss of a loved one or the prospect of our own long and lingering death, we raise the agonizing question, where is God now?

The prophet Isaiah—in the midst of national apostasy, political collapse, and divine judgment concludes, "Truly you are a God who hides himself" (Isaiah 45:15). To say God is hidden, of course, does not mean that He is absent. On the contrary, someone who is hidden is actually present, just not seen. The child who is hiding in the room is certainly there. God conceals Himself, often in things that we would least expect—a crucified criminal, a book, water, bread, wine, a gouty pastor, trials and suffering, human beings working and raising their families.

The hiddenness of God is one of the most profound themes in Lutheran spirituality. It is part of what is termed "the theology of the cross," which might be better thought of as the spirituality of the cross. It has to do with Christ's work, His presence, and how we draw closer to Him. The theology of the cross also deals with the difficulties and hardships that Christians must live through in an utterly realistic and honest way.

THE THEOLOGY OF THE CROSS VS. THE THEOLOGY OF GLORY

In the "spirituality" section of most bookstores, one will find shelves and shelves of titles offering a whole array of techniques and teachings that will solve all problems and bring us to the pinnacle of success. Meditation, the physical disciplines of yoga, pop psychology, principles of positive thinking—all promise empowerment. Not only will they bring personal peace and happiness, if rightly applied, they promise to improve one's physical health, from losing weight to conquering cancer. Spiritual disciplines are also put forward as methods for career advancement, to the point that business books often seem indistinguishable from spiritual books (what with their positive-thinking mantras to help score big sales and their fire-walking, "imaging" techniques). Some books speak of actualizing the self to the point that the self is spoken of in terms traditionally reserved for God. The self becomes the Creator ("you create your own reality") and the Lawgiver ("you determine what's right for you"), eliminating the need for a Redeemer. New Age spirituality affirms that the *Self* is, in fact, God, and that all things, if we could only realize it, share the same divine unity. In much of today's pop religions, "spirituality" becomes a means to a more worldly end, or to the end of enhancing the self— acquiring power, pleasure, and in some cases self-deification.

What is true of the New Age racks can also be found in Christian bookstores. Today their shelves too are stocked with ways of using God for one's own health, happiness, and prosperity. There are Christian diet books, titles on the "Management Techniques of Jesus Christ," and analyses of Christ as the master salesman. Other books deal with more serious concerns, offering solutions for child-raising problems and improving society. Their covers make vast and excited claims, as if by following certain steps family problems will disappear, our bodies will do what we want, our financial problems will evaporate, we will solve our nation's problems, grow the church, and live happily ever after.

Certainly, the Bible has much to say about how we should live, and its wisdom can shape our family lives and cultural issues in profound ways. In fact, as the next chapter on *vocation* will show, the Christian faith has implications for the apparently secular work of managers, salesmen, and, above all, parents.

But the problem with the way spirituality merges with self-help is that the various panaceas do not really even do what they claim to do. The best Christian families still experience conflicts, intractable problems, and embarrassing failures. The most devout Christian may go bankrupt, or have a mental breakdown, or contract a heartbreaking disease and not be healed.

The books do not really help then, except to accentuate our sense of failure. Even if their step-by-step spiritual principles are valid, given our inability to keep God's Law, we never consistently follow them. The ideal of the "victorious Christian life" proves impossible to attain, though we have to suppress our failures, keep trying harder (and buying more books), and present a more positive front to the world. We thus resort to dishonesty and phoniness.

Luther called this kind of self-aggrandizing, success-centered, power spirituality "the theology of glory." Of course its attraction is understandable. Naturally we want success, victories, and happiness. We will be attracted to any religion that can promise us such things. We want complete and understandable answers, evidence of tangible spiritual power, all conveyed by an impressive, well-run, and effective institution. Instead, God gives us the cross.

I have heard that missionaries sometimes have a hard time explaining Jesus to followers of tribal faiths. "Our god is a great warrior," they sometimes respond. "He would not let himself be killed like your Jesus." The *theology of the cross* cuts against the grain of all natural religion, all of what we expect and want in a spiritual system. God manifested Himself not as an abstract principle, but He came down from heaven. Not as sheer energy, but as a baby. He was born, in a rather scandalous way, of a poor virgin, not in a king's palace, but in a stable for animals. To be sure, the angels celebrated His coming, but they announced it not to the king, but to shepherds. Throughout His life, the Son of God emptied Himself of glory (Philippians 2:6–8).

To be sure, this Jesus was powerful, healing the sick and ruling nature itself, but He remained unpopular, scorned, homeless ("foxes have holes and birds of the air have nests, but the Son of Man has no place to lay his head" [Matthew 8:20]). As prophesied,

> He had no beauty or majesty to attract us to him, nothing in his appearance that we should desire him. He was despised and rejected by men, a man of sorrows, and familiar with suffering. Like one from whom men hide their faces he was despised, and we esteemed him not. (Isaiah 53:2–3)

Strange for the Son of God to come like this. And then this Jesus was arrested, tried, and executed, nailed to a cross. The prophet continues:

> Surely he took up our infirmities and carried our sorrows, yet we considered him stricken by God, smitten by him, and afflicted. But he was pierced for our transgressions, he was crushed for our iniquities; the punishment that brought us peace was upon him, and by his wounds we are healed. We all, like sheep, have gone astray, each of us has turned to his own way; and the LORD has laid on him the iniquity of us all. (Isaiah 53:4–6)

In this chapter of the Old Testament—not the New, as one might expect—Isaiah foresees how Christ's weakness impacts our own weakness. On the cross, He carried not only our transgressions and our iniquity, but "our infirmities" and "our sorrows."

The rest of the story is that Christ rose from the dead. He ascended back into the glory that was His. And, in the words of the Nicene Creed, "He shall come again with glory."[1] And His followers will live in glory. We really will live happily ever after. But in the meantime, while we live on this earth, there is the cross.

"If anyone would come after me," Jesus said, "he must deny himself and take up his cross daily and follow me" (Luke 9:23). Conversely, "anyone who does not carry his cross and follow me cannot be my disciple" (Luke 14:27). This by no means implies that we have to suffer as Jesus did, much less that suffering is some sort of meritorious act or payment for our sins. Jesus did all of that for us. It does mean that the spiritual life has to do with suffering, defeat, and weakness—not simply with the experience of "glory" as we might like.

It also, however, implies a peculiar way that Jesus relates to us. Coming to faith, as we have seen, involves being broken by the Law, coming to grips with our moral failure. Legalistic religions, in which one saves oneself by one's own efforts, are very specifically *theologies of glory*, optimistically assuming success and glorifying the powers of the successful, virtuous person. But when we realize just how lost we are, then we cling to the cross, trusting Christ to do for us what we cannot do for ourselves. This is saving faith, the *theology of the cross*.

In ordinary life, we still have our problems, but these too are related to Christ. Our crosses are connected to His.

BEARING THE CROSS

One of the best books on the theology of the cross is by Richard Eyer, who for years served as a hospital chaplain, ministering to the sick and the dying. In *Pastoral Care Under the Cross*, Pastor Eyer tells of a patient, Mr. Witti, who required kidney dialysis and was in intensive care following open-heart surgery. Whenever Pastor Eyer would pray with him—asking that God's will would be done—Mr. Witti, following a common Lutheran custom, would make the sign of the cross.

When his daughter visited him, however, she would be all smiles, bubbling over with reassurances, telling her father not to worry, that God would heal him. "But somehow her father doesn't seem comforted by this," Pastor Eyer recalls, "and turns to me to make the sign of the cross." The daughter believes that having enough faith will lead to healing. "There is no place for weakness and suffering in her understanding of the will of God." But while she is busy trying to get God to surrender to her will, her father has surrendered to the will of God. "He knows that it is the cross that lies at the heart of one's confidence in the Lord."[2]

"As much as parishioners may want to see the hand of God in nature's beautiful sunrises, moving stories of conversion, or success in parish programs," observes Pastor Eyer, "it is in the cross of Christ and in bearing their own crosses that God chooses to reveal his heart to them." With the theology of glory, "we will begin to demand that God justify himself to us in our sufferings by giving us healing and success. We will demand a God who does what we want him to do, and we will reject the way of the cross by which He comes to us. We will become fearful of suffering and preoccupied with its avoidance at the expense of truth and faithfulness."[3]

In the hospital, patients are helpless. They are dependent—on the medical staff, on medication, on machines. Many sick people hate the thought of being dependent on life-support equipment, preferring even death to being "hooked up on some machine." Our culture also draws away from people who are utterly dependent. Those who believe in physician-assisted suicide hold that it is better to die than to suffer or to be dependent. Those who believe in euthanasia maintain that a life of dependence, weakness, and suffering is not worth living, that at some point it is a kindness for those who are sick to be killed.

Being helpless and utterly dependent, however, is precisely our spiritual condition. We are utterly helpless to save ourselves. We are utterly dependent on God. Saving faith involves giving up on our pretensions of being self-sufficient, strong, and in control. Instead, we are to rest in utter dependence on Jesus Christ. "My grace is sufficient for you," the Lord told St. Paul, "for my power is made perfect in weakness" (2 Corinthians 12:9).

It is natural for us to want to save ourselves, to cultivate a spiritual independence and self-sufficiency, so that we can be in control of our spiritual lives. No wonder we have such a fondness for religions of Law, theologies of glory, which allow us to center on our own achievements, merits, and accomplishments. That we keep failing to achieve, merit, and accomplish what we think we should—however we evade our failures by rationalization or dishonesty—by no means alters the goal of spiritual self-sufficiency. In a truly evangelical spirituality, however, this attitude must be broken, so that we awake to our need and put our trust in Christ rather than in ourselves. In the Gospel, our sense of independence is replaced by a sense of dependence.

It is also natural for us to desire independence, self-sufficiency, and control in our earthly lives, to prefer death to dependence, to judge our own worth and those of others in terms of the capacity to do, as it were, "good works." Such attitudes may have their value, as will be seen, in the secular sphere. Still, even in secular terms, the members of a family are supposed to be dependent on each other, as are the members of a society or of an economic system. The attitude of complete self-sufficiency cannot only undermine faith, it can wreck God's design for human relationships.

Just as such complacency is shattered by the Law, in everyday life such complacency is shattered by bearing the cross—that is, by failure, frustration, disappointment, difficulties, struggles, and suffering. Both the Law and the cross drive us to an ever-deeper and more-intimate dependence on Jesus Christ, who meets our sin and our sufferings in His cross.

THE HIDDEN LIFE

It has been said that contemporary Christians lack a theology of suffering. We, understandably, want to avoid it at all costs—and yet it comes, but we do not know what to do with it or what it means.

The fact of suffering is often taken as a sign that there cannot be a God. An all-loving, all-powerful God would not allow suffering to take place, people assume, but would make everyone happy. And since the world does contain so much suffering, God must not exist. Even worse, the fact of suffering is sometimes taken to mean that the sufferer has been rejected by God. The assumption is that Christians will not suffer, that if one has enough faith, God will grant healing, prosperity, and success. Such is our penchant for theologies of glory that whole churches are built today around promises of good health and financial success, not only through following biblical principles but from "name it and claim it" acts of faith. The Lutheran evangelical theology of the cross offers a theology of suffering, but more than that, it offers a practical, realistic, and spiritually-dynamic paradigm for the Christian life.

First, it must be emphasized that the theology of the cross, while it speaks of the spiritual significance of suffering, by no means advocates suffering as a means of spiritual enlightenment. The theology of the cross is not asceticism, the purposeful cultivation of unpleasant experiences so as to gain spiritual merit or some salutary mortification of the flesh. The elaborate mortifications practiced by many in the world's religions—fastings, scourges, self-torment—may involve suffering, but they are still to be classified in the theology of glory, with their heroic acts of self-denial and self-control. Lutherans, though many practice Lenten disciplines, are almost never ascetic. Our cross, Luther taught, is never self-chosen, never self-imposed. Any crosses we choose for ourselves can hardly have much of an effect. Rather, bearing one's cross has to do precisely with the suffering that we do not choose for ourselves, the trials and difficulties that are imposed on us from the outside, that we have no control over whatsoever.[4]

Nor does cross-bearing necessarily involve the dramatic suffering of the cancer patient or the bereft parent, though it may. Bearing the cross often has to do more with the petty, ordinary obstacles and frustrations of everyday life and, as a later chapter will show, with troubles in one's vocation. Boredom, mild depression, and bad moods can be crosses, no less than physical pain and emotional turmoil.

Whether the problems are dramatic or mundane, they are all "trials." However much we, understandably, try to avoid them, trials are an inevitable part of everyone's life. The theology of the cross teaches how they also play an important role in the life of faith.

It must be emphasized that the theology of the cross does not offer some pat answer for suffering, some new theodicy that offers a new explanation for why God allows bad things to happen. For Luther, struggling with the "why" is at the essence of trial. Luther even speaks of trial as struggling with God. Sometimes it may seem that God is contradicting Himself, as when a pastor finds God seemingly thwarting the very ministry to which he has been called. Luther cites Abraham's struggle with God's seemingly contradictory commands when he was told to sacrifice his son, and observes how Jacob literally wrestled with God.[5]

"The most severe trial," says Walther von Loewenich, quoting Luther, "comes upon a person when he believes he has been forsaken and rejected by God. Such a trial comes only to the 'greatest of saints.'"[6] Ironically, what in many traditions would be a sign of spiritual failure—doubting one's election, feeling God's absence—for Luther is a sign of the greatest sanctity, reserved (thankfully) for the spiritual giants.

"What kind of advice can Luther give in such cases? None other than that one must cling to the Word. And the Word, for Luther, is nothing else than Christ."[7] Over and over in his writings, Luther tells those who are doubting whether they have been saved, those who question whether God loves them, those who think they have committed a sin that God will not forgive, to read God's promises in the Bible and to hold Him to His Word—to remember the objective fact that they have been baptized—to receive Christ's body and blood in Holy Communion—to cling to the cross of Jesus Christ.

To believe in God's Word of promise, despite one's feelings, is faith. This is why all trials, both major and small, are occasions for the exercise of faith. "We live by faith, and not by sight" (2 Corinthians 5:7). In the darkness, when we cannot see, we can only listen for God's voice, whereupon we can draw closer to the hidden God.

Another reason trials can have a salutary spiritual effect is that they drive us to prayer. In moments of desperation—when we know in a panic that we cannot control what is happening, in a car wreck, in a cancer diagnosis, when a loved one is fighting for her life—we turn instinctively to prayer. Even nonbelievers do. For a Christian, those moments of need bring out our utter dependence upon God, a realization at the heart of faith. When we are in desperate need, we pray with an intensity, a heartfelt passion, that is particularly genuine and authentic. "Prayer like this," says

Gustaf Wingren quoting Luther, "can hardly be made by anyone who is not in deep need and desperation. 'For what sort of prayer would it be if need were not present and pressing upon us?' "[8] Again, crying out to God in the depths of one's need is an act of faith and an occasion in which the hidden God who answers prayers draws closer.

How this all plays out in ordinary life, how faith and prayer and the hiddenness of God transform day-to-day living, will be the subject of the next chapter. For now, it must be remembered that though God is hidden—that is, He cannot be seen or experienced—in the crosses we bear, He is nevertheless genuinely present, a real presence grasped by faith.

Furthermore, the Christian's spiritual life is itself hidden. "For you died," says St. Paul, "and your life is now hidden with Christ in God. When Christ, who is your life, appears, then you also will appear with him in glory" (Colossians 3:3–4). Having been buried with Christ in Baptism and having been joined with His cross in faith, the Christian's life is "hidden." At the resurrection of the dead and the eternal life in heaven, there will of course be no crosses, God will be clearly manifest in everything, and then will be the time for glory. But for now, the Christian's life is hidden with Christ.

So far we have spoken of justification, but said little about sanctification, the process by which a Christian grows in holiness. The next chapter will speak about good works and action in the world. But the relationship between the human being and God is wholly a matter of faith, not human works, and a large part of sanctification is growing in faith. This comes, again, by trial and the cross, in which the struggles of life force us to grow in our dependence on God and thus cause us to grow in our faith. Good works, as will be seen, are a spontaneous result of faith. Those who need to do more good works need more faith, a deeper apprehension of the Gospel, in order to produce them.

But sanctification, spiritual growth, is no smooth progress. Whether we consider growth in faith or growth in good works, both of which are implicit in the doctrine of sanctification, the holiness of a Christian is not always evident. Failures, hypocrisies, doubts, lack of love, apathy, phoniness, egotistical pride, and secret sins of the flesh are well-documented in Christian churches.

The church, in fact, often seems like a rather weak and attenuated institution. Christians, or churchgoers, often seem little different from their non-Christian neighbors. Individual Christians usually have to admit these charges in their own lives, and in fact they confess them daily. Their relationship with God often seems to vacillate wildly, from times of ecstatic closeness to God to times when He seems absent, from times of spiritual energy to periods of spiritual dryness. Often, little progress is evident, just one failure, followed by a fresh start, followed by another failure. If God is really at work in the lives of Christians, shouldn't one expect better than this?

Luther speaks much of how our "old man" is in conflict with our "new man." The baptized, converted sinner is given a new spiritual nature, a new life in Christ through the indwelling Holy Spirit. But the old sinful nature, inherent in our fallen flesh, remains (see Galatians 5:16–26). These are in conflict, so that the Christian may still succumb to his sinful flesh, which in turn must be disciplined and resisted, while the "new man" is to grow in faith and love. Only at death, when the flesh passes away, will this conflict be resolved, with the regenerated nature attaining full perfection when it enters eternal life.

But in the meantime, the new man is hidden. This is not just a matter—much less an excuse—of Christians failing in their calling. Their true identity and status before God is hidden even to themselves. Again, God sees Christians through the prism of the cross: Our sins and failures are hidden by the blood of Christ; our ordinary lives are hidden, and we are robed by Christ's righteousness. When God looks at a Christian, He sees Jesus.

As St. Paul says, our lives are hidden "with Christ." Our sins are hidden in the cross. Our righteousness is hidden in His. Our lives are hidden, in effect, from God. They are certainly hidden from ourselves and from the world.

This is the basis for our spiritual security. The Christian's life is safely hidden away. Though Lutherans believe in the Law's message that a Christian refusing to repent of sin and rejecting the faith can fall away, the Gospel banishes all fear.

"The wind blows wherever it pleases," says Jesus Himself. "You hear its sound, but you cannot tell where it comes from or where it is going. So it is with everyone born of the Spirit" (John 3:8). God's Spirit is at work in the lives of every Christian, mysteriously changing the heart, acting with Word and Sacrament, ministering in trials and tribulations, creating someone who will stand before God in heaven as *holy*. But this process cannot be evident to the naked eye, nor can it be measured and tracked, nor is the Christian himself necessarily conscious of how far he has come.

The average church member may not seem very impressive. His faults are evident. He may lose his temper, be prone to gossip, and have a worldly streak. He may not even seem very spiritual. And yet, his life is hidden with Christ in God. Every Sunday he hears God's Word of judgment and forgiveness. He examines himself and steps up to the altar to receive Christ's body and blood given for him. He may not always be the best husband, but when his wife dies, he cries out in misery to God. Such folks often say little, but then exhibit a startlingly powerful faith when the chips are down.

It is common today to question whether churchgoers are "really Christians" and to dismiss "dead churches" because we expect spiritual dynamos. To be sure, church rolls may include nonbelievers, there are churches that no longer preach the Gospel and so are dead (despite their high membership totals), and there are spiritual giants that put the rest of us to shame. Nevertheless, to paraphrase C. S. Lewis, the average man or woman in the pew may, to God, be a blessed saint before whom, if we only knew, we would have the impulse to bow down. We just cannot judge by appearances.

Nor can we judge by appearances when we experience suffering or when God seems distant or rejecting, or not real at all. Nor can we judge by appearances when considering what is happening when water, bread, and wine are used in a church service, or when the pastor reads from a book and proclaims words from a pulpit. If we were to judge from appearances, we would scarcely have thought that this Jewish carpenter is actually God in the flesh. His being tortured to death at Golgotha, judged strictly by appearances, would be repulsive, a meaningless act of cruelty. We would never guess that it was the salvation of the whole world.

NOTES

[1] In *The Book of Concord*, 18.

[2] Richard C. Eyer, *Pastoral Care Under the Cross: God in the Midst of Suffering* (St. Louis: Concordia Publishing House, 1994), 26.

[3] Ibid., 27–28.

[4] See Gustaf Wingren, *Luther on Vocation* (Evansville, IN: Ballast Press, 1994), 52–53.

[5] Walther von Loewenich, *Luther's Theology of the Cross* (Minneapolis: Augsburg, 1982), 136–37.

[6] Ibid., 136.

[7] Ibid., 137.

[8] Wingren, 189.

vocatioN

....

THE SPIRITUALITY OF ORDINARY LIFE

There is another place where God is hidden: in everyday life. The ordinary routine of making a living, going shopping, being a good citizen, and spending time with one's family, are spheres in which God is at work, through human means. Luther described the various occupations—parenthood, farming, laborers, soldiers, judges, retailers, and the like—as all being "masks of God."

Luther's doctrine of "vocation" may be one of his most original contributions to understanding the spiritual life. If he is critical of mystical ascents to the divine, insisting instead that God descends to the sinner in the means of grace, Luther goes on to lay the groundwork for what might be called a mysticism of ordinary life. If he denies that salvation is a result of our good works, insisting that forgiveness is a free gift, Luther's doctrine of vocation gives good works a very different spiritual significance. If he sometimes minimizes human beings as radically sinful and limited, in his doctrine of vocation, he exalts human beings to a startling degree. In the doctrine of vocation, spirituality is brought down to earth to transfigure our practical, everyday life.

Today, more than in Luther's time, we define ourselves by our work. Our busy schedules, our multiple commitments, the ways we are pulled in so many directions at once, often leave us exhausted. It is not always clear if our priorities are right, or if any of it is worthwhile. Work often seems detrimental to the spiritual life, involving moral compromises, "worldly" priorities, and neglect of our families. The pressures of work, including when we fail or are not as successful as we want to be, also can be paralyzing. And yet, work, of one kind or another, remains at the center of our lives, the locus of our ambitions and accomplishments.

"What are you going *to be* when you grow up?" we ask even young children, and we do not have in mind something on the order of "a nice person" or "someone who enjoys nature" or "a person with many hobbies." We have in mind a job. "I *am* a teacher," we say, or "a machinist" or "an executive assistant." Our very being is tied up in our job description.

To be sure, this conflating of our very selves with our work can be a perverse confusion. We can use our work as a pretext for neglecting what are perhaps more important offices we also hold, such as "I am a spouse" or "I am a parent" or "I am a citizen." Those who do not get paid for what they do, but who nevertheless do priceless work—such as housewives and full-time parents—are made to feel out of synch, as are retired people. Work becomes a mad status game, as we measure one job against another, and value people based on the prestige of their jobs. Nevertheless, we cannot help making work—of some kind—a benchmark of who we are.

In the meantime, in our, as we say, workaday world, we are preoccupied by other issues, by questions about how to have a good family and how we should raise our children. We are caught up in economic issues, needing more money and spending it on things we need and like. We are affected by politics, by the responsibilities and frustrations of citizenship, by governmental policies and the legal system.

All of these arenas—which consume most of life—are illuminated and given significance and direction when they are seen in terms of the doctrine of vocation.

MASKS OF GOD

God is sovereign over every aspect of His creation. He did not just create the universe in one big bang, then let it run on its own. He keeps it in existence, "sustaining all things through his powerful word" (Hebrews 1:3). God governs and is intimately involved in everything that He has made, that is, everything that exists. This sovereignty includes the laws of physics and the motions of galaxies, the affairs of nations and the fall of a sparrow (Matthew 10:29), and His providence extends over nonbelievers no less than believers.

Lutheran theology speaks of *two kingdoms*, that God rules both the spiritual and the earthly realm, though in different ways. This notion will be discussed in the next chapter, but for now it is important to remember that God is the king of them both. In both His spiritual and His earthly kingdoms, God is active, and He works through means. In the spiritual realm, He works, as we have seen, through the Word and the Sacraments. In the earthly realm, He rules through *vocation*.

In the Lord's Prayer, we ask that God give us our daily bread, which He does. He does so, not directly as with the manna to the

Israelites, but through the work of farmers, truck drivers, bakers, retailers, and many more. In fact, He gives us our daily bread through the functioning of the whole accompanying economic system—employers and employees, banks and investors, the transportation infrastructure and technological means of production—each part of which is interdependent and necessary, if we are going to eat. Each part of this economic food chain is a vocation, through which God works to distribute His gifts.

God heals the sick. While He can and sometimes does do so directly, in a spectacular unmediated miracle, in the normal course of things God heals through the work of doctors, nurses, and other medical vocations. God protects us from evil. This He does by means of the vocation of police officers, attorneys, judges—also through the military vocations. God teaches through teachers, orders society through governments, proclaims the Gospel through pastors.

Luther pointed out that God could have decided to populate the earth by creating each individual and each generation separately, from the dust. Instead, He invented families. God ordained that new life come into the world—and be cared for and raised into adulthood—through the work of a man and a woman who come together into a family. Husband, wife, father, mother are vocations through which God extends His creation and exercises His love.[1]

All of this simply demonstrates that, in His earthly kingdom, just as in His spiritual kingdom, God bestows His gifts through means. God ordained that human beings be bound together in love, in relationships and communities existing in a state of interdependence. In this context, God is providentially at work caring for His people, each of whom contributes according to his or her God-given talents, gifts, opportunities, and stations. Each thereby becomes what Luther terms a "mask of God":

> All our work in the field, in the garden, in the city, in
> the home, in struggle, in government—to what does it
> all amount before God except child's play, by means of
> which God is pleased to give his gifts in the field, at
> home, and everywhere? These are the masks of our Lord
> God, behind which he wants to be hidden and to do all
> things.[2]

God, who pours out His generosity on the just and the unjust, believer and unbeliever alike, hides Himself in the ordinary social functions and stations of life, even the most humble. To use another of Luther's examples, God Himself is milking the cows through the vocation of the milkmaid.[3]

All of the vocations are thus channels of God's love. Gustaf Wingren, the Swedish theologian who authored the classic book on the subject, summarizes the point:

> In his vocation man does works which effect the
> well-being of others; for so God has made all offices.
> Through this work in man's offices, God's creative work
> goes forward, and that creative work is love, a profusion
> of good gifts. With persons as his "hands" or "cowork-
> ers," God gives his gifts through the earthly vocations,
> toward man's life on earth (food through farmers, fisher-
> men and hunters; external peace through princes,
> judges, and orderly powers; knowledge and education
> through teachers and parents, etc., etc.). Through the
> preacher's vocation, God gives the forgiveness of sins.
> Thus love comes from God, flowing down to human
> beings on earth through all vocations, through both spir-
> itual and earthly governments.[4]

Thus, God is graciously at work, caring for the human race through the work of other human beings. Behind the care we have received from our parents, the education we received from our teachers, the benefits we receive from our spouse, our employers, and our government lurks God Himself, bestowing His blessings.

The picture is of a vast, complex network of human beings with different talents and abilities. Each serves the other. Each is served by others. We Americans have an ideal of self-sufficiency and often dream of being able to grow our own food, build our own homes, and live independently of other people. But our proper human condition, once again, is *dependence*. Because of the centrality of love, we are to depend on other human beings and, ultimately and through them, on God. Conversely (and eliminating the welfare syndrome), other people are to depend on us. We are to work for the good of other people. In God's earthly kingdom, we are to receive His blessings from other people in their vocations, and they, in turn, are to be blessed through us.

Before I became a Lutheran and before I studied the doctrine of vocation, I had the bad habit of always trying to do home repairs on my own, without having the remotest ability to do so. The result was always frustration, wasted time, and bungled jobs, plus higher repair bills than they would normally have been. Attempts to fix an electrical outlet would only result in a hole in the wall and almost getting myself killed. I now realize my problem: I have no vocation for that sort of thing.

Today I joyfully draw on the vocation of plumbers, electricians, and carpenters—also auto mechanics, barbers, cooks, bankers, and artists. Individuals who do have do-it-yourself talents should by all means use them; having such diverse abilities is itself a gift from God, a collection of callings. But the point is, in our earthly lives, we do not have to do everything. Earthly life—and this is operative with non-believers no less than believers—consists of giving and receiving, serving and being served, in a network of economic and social and personal interdependence.

The task of serving as a *mask of God* is a daunting one, defining as it does the scope and nature of Christian service. "God bestows all that is good on us," says Luther, "but. . .you must work and lend yourself as a means and a mask to God."[5]

HAVING A CALLING

The word "calling," or in its Latinate form "vocation," had long been used in reference to the sacred ministry and the religious orders. Certainly, the pastoral office is a crucial vocation, a distinctly functioning "mask of God." But the Lutherans were the first to use "vocation" to refer also to secular offices and occupations. Today, the term has become commonplace, another synonym for a profession or job, as in "vocational training." But behind the term is the notion that every legitimate kind of work or social function is a distinct "calling" from God, requiring unique God-given gifts, skills, and talents.

The purpose of one's vocation, whatever it might be, is serving others. It has to do with fulfilling Christ's injunction to love one's neighbor. Though justification has nothing to do with good works, vocation does involve good works. The Christian's relationship to God is based on sheer grace and forgiveness on God's part; the Christian's relationship to other people, however, is to be based on love put into action. As Wingren puts it, "God does not need our good works, but our neighbor does."[6]

The person who has been justified by faith, who realizes the forgiveness of Christ and who is thereby changed by the Holy Spirit, is motivated by love, not by the rules and regulations and threats of the Law. The good works which follow, however, are not done, as is often piously said, "for God," but for other people. Strictly speaking, we do not "serve God"—rather, He is always the one serving us; instead, we serve our neighbors.

Luther goes so far as to say that works done supposedly for God alone, and not for the benefit of actual human beings, lose their moral value:

> If you find yourself in a work by which you accomplish something good for God, or the holy, or yourself, but not for your neighbor alone, then you should know that that work is not a good work. For each one ought to live, speak, act, hear, suffer, and die in love and service for another, even for one's enemies, a husband for his wife and children, a wife for her husband, children for their parents, servants for their masters, masters for their servants, rulers for their subjects and subjects for their rulers, so that one's hand, mouth, eye, foot, heart and desire is for others; these are Christian works, good in nature.[7]

For Luther, ascetic self-denials, God-appeasing rituals, and private moralistic attitudes are not good works at all—one must actually help somebody.

Though Lutheranism is often accused of antinomianism, a too-permissive dismissal of the moral law in light of the radical free gift of the Gospel, this is a gross misunderstanding. Our relationship to God is not determined by our good works (since those with a sinful nature can never have enough of them to earn anything before God)—what we need rather, is forgiveness for our sins and the perfect good works of Jesus Christ. But our relationship to our neighbors is determined by our good works, which themselves are only made possible by God working through us. Lutheranism in fact displaces morality from the realm of the theoretical and overly theological, bringing it down into the realm of real life.

Certainly, human beings still sin in vocation.[8] We violate God's law and neglect our responsibilities to love and serve others selflessly in our work and offices. Though we resist God's project of working through us, there is something about vocation itself that makes good things happen to others despite ourselves. There is, in fact, as Wingren shows, a great conflict and irony, between our generally selfish motivations and the way the masked God works in vocation:

> Here we come across what for Luther is the decisive contrast between God's self-giving love and man's ego-centricity. The human being is self-willed, desiring that whatever happens shall be to his own advantage. When husband and wife, in marriage, serve one another and their children, this is not due to the heart's spontaneous and undisturbed expression of love, every day and hour. Rather, in marriage as an institution something compels the husband's selfish desires to yield and likewise inhibits the egocentricity of the wife's heart. At work in marriage is a power which compels self-giving to spouse and children. So it is the "station" itself which is the ethical agent, for it is God who is active through the law on earth.[9]

The vocation of marriage itself causes selfish human beings to care for each other and support each other more than they would on their own. The vocation of parenthood causes normally selfish adults to sacrifice their own needs for the well-being of their children. And this is usually done not as a legalistic obligation, but as something parents want to do, that they do spontaneously, for their children.

By the same token, the owner of a company may have no interest whatsoever in loving his neighbor or serving others. His sole motivation may be greed. And yet, because of his vocation, he manages to give jobs to his employees so that they can support their families, his company provides products that other people need or enjoy, making him, however inadvertently, a blessing to his neighbors. Our own sinful inclinations do not necessarily thwart the way God works in vocation.

How do we know our vocation? Strictly speaking—and contrary to the way we pressure young people to "decide" what they are going to do when they grow up—a vocation is not something we choose for ourselves. Rather, it is given by God, who "calls" us to a particular work or station. God gives each individual unique talents, skills, and inclinations. He also puts each individual in a unique set of external circumstances, which are understood as having been providentially arranged by God. Since vocation is not self-chosen, it can be known too through the actions of others. Getting offered a job, being elected to an office, finding someone who wants to marry you, are all clues to vocation.

Essentially, your vocation is to be found in the place you occupy in the present. A person stuck in a dead-end job may have higher ambitions, but for the moment, that job, however humble, is his vocation. Flipping hamburgers, cleaning hotel rooms, emptying bedpans all have dignity as vocations, spheres of expressing love of neighbor through selfless service, in which God is masked. Perhaps later, another vocation will present itself. But vocation is to be found not simply in future career decisions, but in the here and now. Nor can a person use the excuse of "not having a vocation for marriage" for getting a divorce, or claim "not having a vocation for parenthood" as a way to dump childrearing responsibilities. If you are married, that's your vocation. If you have children, they are your vocation.

Vocations are also multiple.[10] Any given person has lots of vocations. A typical man might be, all at the same time, a husband (serving his wife), a father (serving his children), a son (serving his still-living parents), an employer (serving his workers), an employee (serving his bosses), a citizen (serving his country). Notice how a person at a particular job can be both a "master," charged with supervising subordinates, and, at the same time, a "servant," answerable to superiors, whether CEOs or stockholders or voters. Leadership and submission may both be called for, as the different vocations make their claims. The doctrine of vocation helps sort out and gives dignity and significance to each of the roles we are asked to play.

ACTING IN, AND OUT OF, VOCATION

Different vocations have their own kinds of authority and spheres of action, and they operate under different rules. It would be the grossest immorality for someone to make perfect strangers take off their clothes and then cut them open with a knife. But this is permissible for someone who is carrying out the vocation of being a doctor.[11] Having sex is immoral outside of marriage, but it is a great good within the vocation of marriage.

When someone injures us, our impulse is to take personal revenge, which is sharply forbidden by Scripture. Punishing crimes—whether this involves high speed chases, shoot-outs, throwing someone in jail, or executing them—simply is not our vocation. This is, however, the vocation of police officers, judges, and the rest of the legal system: "Do not take revenge, my friends," writes St. Paul, "but leave room for God's wrath, for it is written: 'It is mine to avenge; I will repay,' says the Lord" (Romans 12:19). Rather, the next verses emphasize that we should forgive those who wrong us, feeding our enemies when they are hungry and overcoming evil with good (12:20–21). But this segues right into a discussion of the role of earthly authorities and the need to submit to them: "for there is no authority except that which God has established" (13:1). The earthly ruler "is God's servant to do you good. But if you do wrong, be afraid, for he does not bear the sword for nothing. He is God's servant, an agent of wrath to bring punishment on the wrongdoer" (13:4). This to say, we are not supposed to take revenge ourselves. This is God's job. But He works through earthly vocations, His "agents" whose vocation involves bearing the sword.[12]

A major controversy in Luther's time was whether a Christian could be a judge, an executioner, or a soldier. After all, the Bible says, "Thou shalt not kill." A judge might have to apply the death penalty, and an executioner has to carry it out. And soldiers in battle are called on to kill—not forgive—their enemies. Luther said that it is certainly true that Christians should not take another's life. God, however, does have the authority to take human life. He does so through the special, lawful vocations of judges, executioners, and soldiers. In a treatise entitled *Whether Soldiers Too Can Be Saved* (1526), Luther concludes that being a soldier is, in fact, a way of serving and loving one's neighbors. In their personal relationships as Christians, soldiers are to forgive their own enemies, but in protecting their country, their vocation allows them to fight and even kill on the battlefield. Being a soldier, in fact, is "a blessed order," a ministry of love:

> So, because it is from God that a soldier receives his fitness to do battle, he may serve therewith, serving with his skill and craft whoever desires his services; and he may accept wages for his labor. For his too is a vocation which issues from the law of love.[13]

Similarly, I would argue that since a father's vocation includes protecting his family, he may use force to do so. But a doctor's vocation is to heal, not kill (ruling out euthanasia). A mother's vocation is to nurture her children (ruling out abortion).

Some might think that such a high view of governing authorities and even the military opens the door for tyranny. As the next chapter will show, that is not the case at all. God is the king of both kingdoms, and His Word governs all. Those who sin in their vocations, who violate God's intentions for that vocation and who fail the tests of selfless service and love of neighbor, are answerable to correction and the wrath of God. The point, for now, is that God really does exercise authority through human beings acting in vocation. There is a divine authority in lawful governments. There is also divine authority in parenthood.[14]

A corollary to the notion that each vocation has its divinely-appointed sphere is that problems will arise when people try to act outside of their vocations. Again, consider the spectacle of me trying to repair electrical appliances. When we work outside of our vocations—that is, without regard to our God-given abilities, inclinations, and station in life—we usually fail miserably or, more seriously, violate the moral law.

It is possible—and common—to pursue occupations for which we have no aptitude and thus no vocation. I have had many students who choose their major in college on the basis of which job pays the most, regardless of the gifts God has given them. They turn themselves into accountants or managers or engineers, though they end up hating their work and not being very good at what they are trying to do. Their true vocation might be music or art, but they are trying to be "practical"—as if vocation were self-chosen—and they deny their true God-given gifts to pursue talents they do not really have. There are people in the teaching profession who do not really have gifts that enable them to be good teachers. There are politicians who just are not cut out to be rulers. Though if they are in those stations, they should consider that they do have a calling and a responsibility to do the best they can. They would do better to build on their own specific gifts.

More serious confusions come when those with one vocation trespass on the prerogatives of another vocation. Again, private citizens have no right to "take the law in their own hands." Nor do rulers of the state have the right to take over the rearing of children, which is the vocation of parents. Luther was particularly vehement when earthly rulers presumed to tell pastors what to preach, expressing himself in a way that should put to rest the accusation that he was servile to secular rulers: "You fool," he said, addressing the prince, "you simpleton, look to your own vocation; don't you take to preaching, but let your pastor do that."[15]

THE PASTORAL VOCATION

The office of the pastor, of course, is a special vocation, not merely in God's earthly kingdom but in His spiritual kingdom. Certainly before God, the pastoral vocation is no more meritorious than that of the farmer, the factory worker, or any other secular vocation. Lutheran evangelicals also were the first to promote the notion of "the priesthood of all believers," that all Christians can have a personal access to God through Christ. And yet, Lutheranism has always had a high view of the pastoral office.

In the order of Confession and Absolution, the traditional Lutheran liturgy has the pastor say these words, after the congregation confesses that "we are by nature sinful and unclean": "Upon this your confession, I, by virtue of my office, as a called and ordained servant of the Word, announce the grace of God unto all of you, and in the stead and by the command of my Lord Jesus Christ I forgive you all of your sins in the name of the Father and of the Son and of the Holy Ghost."[16]

Non-Lutherans are often shocked at the notion that the pastor forgives sin, but his ability to do so is simply the proclamation of the Gospel, his ability to "announce the grace of God." He is forgiving sin not by his own powers but in the name of Christ. The members of the congregation can be assured of forgiveness insofar as they have repented ("upon this your confession") and have faith not in the pastor but in God's Word, the Gospel of Christ that he proclaims. Nevertheless, the pastor is a concrete—one might say sacramental—vehicle for that message of forgiveness. Luther's

Small Catechism says that we are to believe the pastor's forgiveness as if it came from Christ Himself. The pastor is acting "in the stead and by the command of my Lord Jesus Christ." That is to say, he is a mask of God.

The implications of the pastor's ministry of Word and Sacrament—and what goes on in church— will be explored further in the next two chapters. For now, it is sufficient to note that the other vocations have to do with God's earthly kingdom; the pastoral office has to do with His spiritual kingdom. The former can wield the sword, said Luther, but the pastor can only wield the Word.[17] Pastors are not ever to use force, to coerce or manipulate anyone into belief; they must trust the power of the Word. They are to preach the Word without compromise, even when it condemns the policies and power systems of the world, but they are never to become merely political, which would trespass upon the vocation of earthly rulers. The pastor's vocation is to call sinners into a kingdom that does not pass away.

It is God who baptizes, through the hands of the pastor. It is Christ who presides over His supper, as the pastor distributes the bread and the wine. It is God's Word that rings out in the pastor's sermon. Lutheran pastors wear robes and vestments and collars to symbolize that this human being—no different in himself from his parishioners—is clothed in an office, in which he must act in the stead and by the command of Christ.

Laypeople too serve in the church, using their abilities and talents—their vocations—for the good of the community of faith. Administering the property, planning events, serving on boards, and the like are necessary for any institution. Laypeople can also proclaim the good news of Christ's forgiveness, primarily operating, again, in their vocation. Parents evangelize their children. At work, relationships are formed with colleagues, who, in the course of friendship and common work, can be introduced to the

Gospel of grace. God's Word extends into the world through vocation. But laypeople—and their pastors—must remember that they do not have to be doing "church work" in order to be working for God. It is easy to spend every night at a church meeting, "doing the Lord's work," but the doctrine of vocation teaches that spending time with your spouse and children and fulfilling the demands of your job are also ways of working for God—or rather, of God working through you.

The vocation of the pastor is to be a "minister"—that is, a servant—of God's Word. He serves us laypeople by feeding us with God's Word and His Sacraments, proclaiming to us God's Law and the Gospel of forgiveness through Jesus Christ. As such, we are highly dependent on our pastors, through whom Christ is conveyed to us. The term "pastor," of course, is simply a term for "shepherd," a humble vocation from God's earthly kingdom. The pastor is charged with taking care of God's sheep. In the pastoral calling, as in all callings, God is hidden.

BEARING THE CROSS IN VOCATION

For all of the exalted spiritual significance in everyday life posited by the doctrine of vocation—how God is present and active in our work and our relationships—it is evident that we often fail, suffer, and experience frustrations in our vocations. Parents may have done everything right towards their children, and yet go through the anguish of having a child turn against them. A business owner's company may go bankrupt, throwing all the employees out of work. A pastor's congregation may turn against him. Problems arise in a marriage. Often or occasionally, vocation turns into a burden, a cross to bear. The theology of the cross applies in particular to vocation.

Since God is at work in vocation, observes Wingren, the devil seeks to thwart vocation. One way is to turn it away from sacrificial service and love of neighbor to a "theology of glory," to self-aggrandizement, pride in good works, and the achievement of a spiritually vacuous success. "Wanting to be exalted instead of serving," says Wingren, "regarding office as a possibility for selfish power instead of for service, is offense against vocation."[18]

Another ploy of the devil is to pry the person out of his or her calling. "Temptation in vocation," says Wingren, "is the devil's attempt to get man out of his vocation."[19] Thus, there may be the temptation to quit: to get a divorce, to leave one's children, to quit the job, to give up writing or making music or whatever talents one has.

Bearing the cross in vocation often involves the sense that one's vocation is worthless or futile. "When the cross of any vocation is borne," says Wingren, "that vocation appears lowly."[20] Ironically, this sensation is experienced even in the vocations that would appear to have the most power and prestige. Presidents and millionaires are often tormented by their responsibilities and by their self-perceived inability to meet them. "Viewed from without," says Wingren, "some offices seem to be surrounded by a pleasing luster. But seen from within, it is evident that those offices too demand sacrificial, downward-reaching service, which is a cross for the old man."[21]

Then there are the ordinary hardships that characterize any vocation. These frustrations and sufferings can become taken into the cross of Christ, however, at precisely the point in which we realize our weakness and our dependence on Christ. The sense of lowliness in vocation can be resisted out of pride, or it can become humility. Our inability to succeed in our own work can bring us to a deeper faith in the God behind the mask.

Trials in vocation drive us to prayer. "He who labors knows that there are times when all human ways are blocked," observes Wingren. "In a special sense this is the time for prayer."[22] When we can handle our own problems through our own ingenuity and effort, there is little need to appeal to God. But when we are at our wits' end, when nothing is working and we are in a state of desperation, then we turn to God. And the most intense, passionate, seeking prayer comes when we are struggling. "For what sort of prayer would it be if need were not present and pressing upon us," says Luther, "that prayer be thereby the stronger?"[23] "Prayer like this," comments Wingren, "potent and transforming, can hardly be made by anyone who is not in deep need and desperation."[24]

And prayer like this is answered. "Desperation arises in our vocation and stimulates prayer. But God's answer to prayer also comes in our vocations; and the divine intervention which answers prayer is closely related to … the transformation of the work of our vocation."[25] Prayer, from our perspective, brings God into our vocation. We commit what we do to God, surrendering to His will and trusting His providence. To cite another remarkable quotation from Wingren, "Prayer is the door through which God, Creator and Lord, enters creatively into home, community, and labor."[26]

Prayer also brings faith to our vocation. The dependence realized in prayer is an example of faith. Without faith, vocations are mere employments, mere things to do, empty of God and empty of meaning. Faith sees them as masks of God. Without faith, suffering is empty and purposeless, an example of the absurdity and meaninglessness of life. With faith, suffering in vocation becomes a cross, comprehended in the saving cross of Jesus Christ.

Wingren concludes:

> Vocation is earthly, just as shockingly earthly as the humanity of Christ, apparently so void of all divinity. In the crucifixion of Christ the divine nature was only hidden, not absent; it was present in the lowly form of love for robbers and soldiers.

> Similarly, God conceals His work of love to men in cross-marked vocation, which is really of benefit to the neighbor. In Christ's victory on the cross, which looks so poor—love's victory in lowliness—God is hidden; therefore the resurrection takes place on the third day. Now Christ's victory is proffered through the Gospel to sorely tried man, who in the labors of his vocation undergoes the crucifixion of his old nature. Through faith in the Gospel, I arise as a new man, born of the church, in hope possessing heaven and eternal life beyond bodily death. From the roughness of earthly life there opens up a vista of life and freedom in the coming kingdom, and only one way leads to it—subjection to the cross here.[27]

NOTES

[1] *Exposition of Psalm 147*, quoted by Gustaf Wingren, *Luther on Vocation* (Evansville, IN: Ballast Press, 1994), 138.

[2] *Exposition of Psalm 147*, quoted by Wingren, 138.

[3] Cited by Wingren, 9.

[4] Wingren, 27–28.

[5] *Exposition of Psalm 147*, quoted by Wingren, 138.

[6] Wingren, 10.

[7] *Adventspostille*, 1522, quoted by Wingren, 120.

[8] And there are some occupations—such as robber, drug dealer, hitman, or pornographer—that are not vocations at all, since they are intrinsically sinful, being incompatible with the love of neighbor, aiming to hurt and corrupt rather than to serve.

[9] Wingren, 6.

[10] See Wingren, 5.

[11] A doctor who does such things outside of his vocation, on the other hand, would still be liable for the crimes of sexual assault or murder.

[12] See Wingren, 7.

[13] Quoted in Wingren, 3–4. See also Wingren's discussion on 7–8, 24–26.

[14] In fact, Luther in the "Small Catechism" derives all earthly authority from the primary authority of parents. See his explanation of the commandment "Honor thy father and thy mother."

15 *Exposition of John 1 and 2*, quoted in Wingren, 114.
16 *The Lutheran Hymnal* (St. Louis: Concordia Publishing House, 1941), 16.
17 See Wingren, 114–15.
18 Wingren, 128.
19 Wingren, 121.
20 Wingren, 130.
21 Wingren, 130–31.
22 Wingren, 185.
23 *The Sermon on the Mount*, quoted in Wingren, 189.
24 Wingren, 189.
25 Wingren, 192.
26 Wingren, 194.
27 Wingren, 57–58.

Living in two kingdoms

THE SACRED AND THE SECULAR

The doctrine of vocation gives spiritual significance to everyday, ordinary life, sanctifying the so-called secular realm of life in this world. Family, work, government, and other dimensions of life in society emerge as arenas of love, service, and the action of God. And yet, the doctrine of justification is otherworldly, marking the deliverance of flawed human beings snared in a sinful world for eternal life in heaven. Lutheran spirituality affirms both truths. As with its other great paradoxes—sin and grace, Law and Gospel, Christ as true God and true man, the Sacrament as mere bread and wine and as the body and blood of Christ—Lutheranism insists that the Christian is a citizen of two different kingdoms at once.

The notion that God has both a spiritual rule and an earthly rule, each of which He rules in different, though related ways, frees Christians to be engaged in the secular realm, without being swept away by secularism. The doctrine of the *two kingdoms* gives a blueprint for Christian activism, while safeguarding against the illusions of political—or theological—utopianism. It transfigures the Christian's life in the world, while safeguarding against worldliness. At one and the same time, the Christian lives in the world through vocation and lives in heaven through faith.

CHRISTIANITY AND CULTURE

The problem of how to live a spiritual life in the midst of an unspiritual world is one of the most vexing dilemmas of the Christian life. Should Christians watch TV, go to the movies, and indulge in other "worldly" pleasures? How different should Christians be from everyone else? Should Christians withdraw from the sinful society or somehow try to reform it? In theology, issues about the proper relationship between faith and culture are dividing churches and confusing their members. Should the church get involved in politics? Do we have the right to impose Christian morality on non-Christians? Should the church change its beliefs and practices to accommodate cultural changes? There are different ways to approach this perennial conflict between the church and the state, the sacred and the secular.

One way to solve the problem is to make religion and culture identical. Most of the world's religions are, quite directly, cultural religions. The spiritual beliefs serve to sanction social practices. In the tribal nature religions, the particular social customs are tied to their gods, explained and justified by mythological tales. In many pagan faiths, the ruler is a god, or descended from a god, and a seamless web is woven to unite nature, culture, and religion into a single whole. Hinduism, with its caste system and rituals, is inextricable from the culture of India. To embrace Islam is to embrace a culture, including details of dress, diet, law, and the Arabic language. It is possible in Judaism, I understand, to be both an atheist and a Jew. For many people, their religion is simply a part of their cultural identity.

The sociological function of religion is so powerful that Christianity too sometimes is reduced to a cultural religion. Orthodox Serbs and Catholic Croats may think religion is important enough to kill each other over it, but I am told that neither side actually goes to church very much. I suspect Northern Ireland harbors atheist Catholics and atheist Protestants, both bent on blowing each other up. In less inflammatory ways, a particular version of Christianity can be reduced to a sign of ethnic identity. This is especially evident in America, with the churches founded by immigrants. We have Polish Catholics and Irish Catholics, German Lutherans and Scandinavian Lutherans, all holding their ethnic festivals in their church parking lots.

To be sure, Christianity can support and influence a particular culture, and cultures are part of God's earthly kingdom and the locus of vocations. But strictly speaking, Christianity is supposed to be a universal, a catholic faith, for individual human beings from all cultures. Jesus charged His people to make disciples and baptize people "of all nations" (Matthew 28:19). The redeemed in heaven include members "of every tribe and tongue and people and nation" (Revelation 5:9)—that is, of every culture.

So if Christianity is not to be coterminous with culture, what is their relationship supposed to be? In his classic book, *Christ and Culture*, H. Richard Niebuhr shows that there are a limited number of possibilities, each of which has been adopted by various Christian theologies.[1]

When some people see a conflict between Christianity and the culture, their impulse is to change Christianity. For them, the culture should rule the church. In a scientific age, the church needs to tone down its supernatural teachings. In a romantic age, the church needs to be more emotional and subjective. If the dominant culture becomes tolerant of extramarital sex, so must the church. This is the response of "liberal theology." It has always taken different forms, depending on the cultural trends of a particular time. The assumption is that the church needs to change as the society changes, in order to be culturally relevant.

In liberal theology, the secular swallows up the sacred. Christianity is reduced to just another cultural religion, and a rather poor and pointless one. Other cultural religions at least lead and influence, but this brand of theological liberalism only follows, in a servile way, the secularist trendsetters. Ironically, though such a view drastically downgrades the supernatural status of the church, such views are the refuge of many clergy and theologians, who worry that their institutions will lose members unless they stay "up to date." Laypeople tend to recognize that if the culture is supreme and the church has nothing different to offer, they might as well just sleep in on Sunday mornings.

Other people, faced with the conflict between their spiritual beliefs and a sinful world, act more heroically. They try to change the world. They plunge into political activism and projects for social reform. Through legislation, political power, and social engineering they believe that society can be reorganized so as to follow God's moral law.

Such activism has a long and often distinguished history, and has been practiced by partisans of both leftwing and rightwing political agendas. When churches turn into political action committees, however, the danger is that they lose their supernatural focus, concentrating instead on earthly programs and becoming just another worldly institution.

And if they should be successful in their project of setting up the perfect society, what would they have? Another divinized culture. Heaven built on earth by human hands is not the same as eternal life. Again, Christianity always has to be more than a cultural religion.

Other Christians respond to the conflicts between their faith and their culture by withdrawing from the sinful world. They separate themselves from secular amusements and institutions. Some take the route of asceticism, denying themselves the pleasures, social involvements, and entertainment options enjoyed by their more secularized neighbors. Others allow themselves entertainment, as long as the music, books, films, and videos have an explicit Christian content. Those for whom the church must be separate from the culture often attempt to set up their own communities along Christian principles. The classic example would be the Amish, who go so far as to reject modern technology in order to keep their community pure. This can also be seen in the Christian commune movement of a few decades ago and in the rise of distinctly Christian businesses and institutions, which constitute a Christian subculture.

Again, there is much to admire here. Christians do need to separate from sin. Self-denial and the rejection of worldliness are genuine virtues. This approach, however, can also become problematic. For one thing, the Bible does call us to service and to action in the world. Pulling back into our Christian enclaves, letting the world, literally, go to hell, is a retreat not easily sanctioned by Scripture. Besides, the resulting subculture tends to acquire cultural problems of its own—the same political games, status seeking, and worldly concerns that characterize the outside culture. The taint of sin that spoils all cultures is not so easily escaped.

Whether the church tries to rule the culture or form a culture of its own, sin runs too deep. None of these schemes are ever successful. Christian monarchies succumb to corruption. Christian communes dissolve due to jealousy, personality conflicts, and overt sin. No one, including Christians, can live a perfectly moral life, much less force anyone else to. And on this fact, all attempts to enshrine a perfectly Christian culture founder.

Whether preaching the need to conform to society, reform it, or separate from it, all of these options are theologies of Law, not Gospel. They reduce Christianity to rules, behavior, and codes of conduct—neglecting the fact that human beings are in such bondage to sin that they *cannot* fulfill the Law. More profoundly, they neglect the fact that Christianity is about God's grace, the atonement of Christ, and the forgiveness of sins. Put another way, in their ambitious kingdom-building, they exhibit the theology of glory, rather than the theology of the cross.

CITIZENS OF TWO KINGDOMS

And yet, there is a validity in both the way of activism and the way of separation from the world. Is it possible to do both? The Bible seems to call for a much more complex stance to the problem of Christianity and culture. When Jesus prayed for His followers, before His arrest in Gethsemane, He set the terms:

> * I have given them your word and the world has hated them, for they are not of the world any more than I am of the world. My prayer is not that you take them out of the world but that you protect them from the evil one. They are not of the world, even as I am not of it. Sanctify them by the truth; your word is truth. As you sent me into the world, I have sent them into the world. (John 17:14–18)

His followers—and He includes not just His disciples but "those who will believe in me through their message" (17:20), namely us—are not "of the world," yet He sends them "into the world." Somehow, Christians must be "in, but not of"—engaged in the world, while still being otherworldly.

In Niebuhr's rehearsal of the various stances Christians have taken to the problem, he describes the Lutheran position as "Christ and culture in paradox." Lutherans call it the doctrine of the *two kingdoms*. According to this view, God does rule the culture, and God does rule the church. But He rules them in two different ways.

According to the Lutheran theology of culture, God is sovereign over all of existence, from the sparrow that falls to the motions of the nebulae, from the inner workings of every individual's conscience to the vast affairs of nations. The so-called secular realms are thus all under His dominion.

Even those who do not believe in God remain under His rule and care. They are under His moral law, which restrains sin and the effects of sin. If the human proclivity for sin were to be fully released, it would tear apart any human relationship. Sin unbound would undercut any sort of cooperation and interdependence that are necessary for any kind of society. Culture would be impossible. God's Law is thus manifest in the restraints of the conscience, external social constraints, legal structures and the moral teachings that all cultures uphold.

All human beings, of all beliefs or lack of beliefs, are also under God's providential care. "He causes his sun to rise on the evil and the good, and sends rain on the righteous and the unrighteous" (Matthew 5:45). And His providential power operates through the normal living and working of human beings. He is masked even in those who do not acknowledge Him. That is to say, He works, as we have seen, through vocation. His whole creation constitutes His kingdom.

God, however, has another kingdom, one of salvation and grace. He relates in a different way to those He reaches down to save, gathering them together in the church, which He guides through the Holy Spirit. God rules His earthly kingdom by power; He rules His spiritual kingdom by love. God's earthly kingdom is under the Law; His spiritual kingdom is under the Gospel.

Christians are citizens of both kingdoms. They are thus to be active members of their cultures, called in vocation to serve their neighbors through moral action. They are also members of Christ's church, justified entirely by faith. In the spiritual kingdom, they are passive recipients of God's grace. In the earthly kingdom, they are active for God in the tasks of their vocations. Christians must function in both realms at once, so that they are "in, but not of" the world.

IMPLICATIONS OF THE TWO KINGDOMS

The doctrine of the two kingdoms does encourage Christian activism. Lutheranism is often accused of encouraging servile obedience to the state. If the ruler's vocation makes him a mask of God, as those Lutherans believe, then resistance to an unjust ruler would be construed as resistance to God. If the secular authorities are part of God's kingdom and if the church is to be purely spiritual, then Lutheranism would seem to keep people from criticizing their leaders or working for social change. Such a view of the two kingdoms is a sheer misunderstanding (even if some Lutherans have had the same misunderstanding). When it comes to social and political structures, God, let it never be forgotten, is the king. While He does work through earthly institutions, they are all subject to His law.

The first use of the moral law is to restrain evil, and this applies specifically to the evils of society. When rulers (or political systems or cultures) violate God's moral law—when they are corrupt, oppressive, or overtly evil—they are in rebellion against God's will and are acting outside of their vocations. When they violate God's law, they are to be called to account. Citizenship itself is a vocation, and Christian citizens are right to criticize evil wherever they see it, including in their leaders, and to work for social, political, and cultural righteousness in the public square.

The contention that Lutheranism tolerates tyranny (including the scurrilous charge that Lutheran social theory allowed the rise of Hitler) has been thoroughly refuted by Uwe Siemon-Netto in his book *The Fabricated Luther*.[2] As I have showed in my own book *Modern Fascism*, Hitler, who rejected the Bible for its Jewishness and who summarized his ideology as "the triumph of the will," was, if not an anti-Christ, at least an anti-Luther. The German church that supported National Socialism had long since embraced the role of cultural religion, teaching that culture rules Christianity and minimizing the Bible's supernatural claims.[3] An orthodox Lutheranism, which upholds the Bible and recognizes "the bondage of the will," must reject—and, in the person and witness of those who confessed their faith did reject—all such culture worship, idolatry, and rebellion against the commandments of God.[4]

A Lutheran perspective on politics, therefore, will be profoundly realistic. It will be very skeptical towards all utopian schemes. No humanly-devised system or institution will be perfect. They all must be subject to moral criticism based on the transcendent, transcultural law of God. At the same time, the doctrine of vocation in God's earthly kingdom validates social, cultural, and political activism. Christian citizens may be under no illusion that they will be able to create heaven on earth through their activism, but they must still uphold and apply God's moral demands.

The doctrine of the two kingdoms actually frees Christians for effective action in the secular arena and untangles the dilemmas they often face in public policy. Morality, for example, is often assumed to be the main business of religion. Thus, those who oppose abortion are accused of trying to impose their religion on others. Invocations of moral principles are routinely ruled out of bounds in a nation that separates church and state. According to Lutheranism, however, morality is the main business not of the church at all, but of the earthly kingdom.

Religion, one's relationship to God, is based not on the Law but the Gospel; but our social relationships with each other are based on the Law. God's moral law is written on the hearts even of non-believers (Romans 2:14–15). The protection of life is the business of all governments, in all cultures, and Christians are right to oppose abortion on moral grounds. This is not imposing *religion* on anyone—that would have to involve forcing people to have faith in Christ, which cannot be done. Christians can work to protect life and uphold other moral principles through pragmatic tactics, cooperating with non-Christian allies, playing politics, and passing laws.

While the doctrine of the two kingdoms allows for activism and engagement in the culture, at the same time, it keeps the church separate and distinct from the world. The church is not to imitate the culture or follow all of its agendas. The church's priority is to proclaim the Gospel, not enforce the Law. Christians are free to participate in their cultures, but not uncritically, recognizing sin and maintaining a certain degree of detachment from the transience of the world. "For here we do not have an enduring city"— we have a city, just not an enduring city—"but we are looking for the city that is to come" (Hebrews 13:14).

CONFUSING THE TWO KINGDOMS

Problems come when the two kingdoms are confused with each other—when the church functions like the culture, or the culture functions like the church. What is appropriate in one realm is often not appropriate in the other. The profit motive works well in economics, and lawbreakers are supposed to be put in prison by the police. But the success of the church is not to be found in the amount of money it makes, and it may not lock people up who disobey its teachings. The church has absolutely no business conducting inquisitions or holy wars.

Trying to "impose" one's religious beliefs on others would indeed be a violation of the Gospel. The church, Luther insisted, may not use coercive power. The church is not allowed to use the sword. Only the Word. "A churchman," says Gustaf Wingren, "must abstain from all earthly weapons, from all coercion and lust for worldly power; for the Word is to use no outward force. The preacher who goes forward, simply trusting in the inner, invisible power of the preached Word, is thus one who is faithful to his vocation."[5] A war may be just and to be fought in one's earthly vocation, but a religious war as such—the notion of conquering people for Christ—is, Luther believed, completely out of order.[6]

Christians, he said, should suffer for their faith, following the cross of Christ, rather than defend their faith through violence. Faith is a gift of God, the work of the Holy Spirit operating through the means of grace. It cannot be imposed on anyone through some act of power or the Sword.

The secular ruler, on the other hand, does employ power, the office of the sword. The lawful secular authorities—not the church—may wage war, coerce obedience, and punish wrongdoers. The secular authorities may not, however, tell pastors what to preach, or otherwise interfere with the office of the Word. They should protect the church, which will not protect itself.

Confusion of the kingdoms also happens when the earthly kingdom tries to ape the workings of the spiritual kingdom. I remember, before I became a Lutheran, listening to a minister argue that the solution to the crime problem is to release all convicted criminals from prison. Jesus said that he had come to proclaim release to the captives, didn't He? If we really believed the Bible, we would take that literally. If we emptied our prisons, the robbers and killers would be so moved that they would reform. Even at the time, that policy proposal seemed rather naive. Now I see that it is also a confusion of the two kingdoms. The earthly kingdom exists to carry out the law; the spiritual kingdom exists to carry out forgiveness. A judge must execute justice, not the unconditional mercy that is found only in the Gospel. To be sure, leniency is possible under the legal system, under certain conditions, but the legal system cannot simply forgive criminals. Christ, of course, can. A criminal might repent, turn to Christ, and receive full forgiveness and acceptance in the church. But a spiritual conversion does not exempt the criminal from being punished by the state.

The kingdoms can also be confused when earthly authorities presume to grant spiritual benefits. Projects that claim to solve all human problems, reform human nature, and eliminate the effects of sin—all through human ideologies and social engineering—may seem well-intentioned, but they are nearly always dangerous. It is a great irony of history that when human beings devise utopian schemes to set up heaven on earth, they come closer to setting up a hell. This was true of the egalitarianism of the French revolution, the state-worship of fascism, the dialectical materialism of communism, and the false promises of every demagogue. Human societies and governments are intrinsically limited, prone to fail, and tainted by sin. They are realms of human and divine service, but they can never be heaven. The only way to heaven is the cross of Jesus Christ.

The church does not depend on power, social prestige, rhetorical manipulation, or human-designed programs. All it has are the Word and Sacraments, which, though they seem weak to the world and to all theologies of glory, in fact carry the life-changing power of the Holy Spirit.

The church—with the Christians who make up the church—is to be otherworldly, focused on the transcendent reality of God's spiritual kingdom, His reign in the human heart and His promise of eternal life. And yet, Christians are also to be engaged in this world in vocation, upholding God's law and playing their part in God's providential control of all of life. Again, both poles of the paradox must be upheld. Religious believers who retreat into a mystical revery, ignoring their responsibilities to serve their neighbors and to act in the world, are neglecting the claims of the earthly kingdom. Religious believers who reject the supernatural claims of faith in favor of social activism and a trust in social progress are neglecting the claims of the spiritual kingdom.

Both kingdoms exist now, at the same time, not as future realities (as if the claims of eternity were only for after death, or as if social morality were only for the future withering away of the state). Every Christian is a citizen of both kingdoms simultaneously and must function both spiritually and in the world. The Christian lives in this tension, often in a state of conflict, since sin and Satan try to ravage and confuse both realms. But God is ultimately sovereign over all that He has made—church and state, believer and non-believer, the sacred and the secular.

EVERYDAY SPIRITUALITY

"A Christian lives in vocation and the church," observes Wingren. "Vocation is the concrete form of the Law, and the church is the concrete form of the Gospel."[7] Both are essential facets of the Christian's life. The person who knows both faith in the Gospel and active service in the world—that is, someone who lives consciously in both kingdoms at once—has a spiritual balance, in which the secular and the sacred, morality and freedom, both have their place.

Luther describes the condition of the ordinary person of humble occupation who knows where he stands in both kingdoms:

> As long as he (e.g. a shoemaker or a blacksmith) clings to these two, to the Word of faith toward God by which the heart is made clean, and to the word of understanding which teaches him how to act toward his neighbor in his station in life, everything is clean to him, even if with his hands and his whole body he deals with nothing but dirt.[8]

The grimy workman is clean in his heart, through faith in Christ. Conversely, everything in his grimy world is clean to him, since this too is part of God's kingdom into which he has been called.

Luther wrote two theological masterpieces that carry seemingly contradictory titles: *The Bondage of the Will*, which emphasizes our slavery to sin, our inability to save ourselves, and our utter dependence on the grace of God; and *The Freedom of the Christian*, in which he explores the utter freedom opened up by faith in Christ. That latter book sets forth two paradoxical theses:

> A Christian is a perfectly free lord of all, subject to none. A Christian is a perfectly dutiful servant of all, subject to all.[9]

The spiritual kingdom is one of perfect freedom, in which kings and peasants, the rich and poor, men and women of all cultures and vocations, are equal before Christ. They are free from the demands of the law and from the demands of the world. And yet, as they live in the earthly kingdom, they *freely* set aside their spiritual freedom for a life of service. Christians voluntarily serve their neighbors, subjugating their own interests for the good of others, living out their vocations in love and good works. Once again, everyday life is transfigured. And faith and good works turn out to be two different sides of the same coin.

We often expect a highly spiritual life to include mystical reveries, superhuman virtue, or the possession of a supernatural power that overcomes all obstacles. Actually, the spiritual life turns out to be somewhat ordinary—on the surface. It involves the universal experiences of forming relationships, marrying and rearing children, struggling with problems, working. The doctrine of the two kingdoms teaches that God is hidden in ordinary, everyday life.

It is thus not simply moments of transcendent ecstasy that are "spiritual." Human relationships are spiritual. The pleasure of being so caught up with someone you love that you forget yourself—as happens so often in marriage—is a high and holy experience. When you act as a parent—protecting, disciplining, caring for, and loving your child—you are intimately close to God, who is hidden and active in what you do for your child.

The satisfaction that we can feel from our work is something spiritual. When you are doing what you do best, when you get so caught up in your work or your art and it is going so well that you are, as they say, in the zone, then God who gave you your talents and your vocation is lurking close in the background.

We also encounter God not only when we serve and work, but when we receive His gifts through others. Being loved by a spouse or a parent or a friend is, in a real sense, being loved by God. Benefiting from the vocations of others—eating a meal in a restaurant, getting your car fixed, going to the doctor, slowing down at the sight of a police officer, buying something well-crafted—are all occasions for thanking God. For me, enjoying a work of art— whether listening to music, reading a novel, or gaping at a painting—is an especially pure example of God's sovereignty in human vocation. That I am able to take such unmerited pleasure through the God-given talents of other people, who have a vocation that I by no means have myself, always fills me with a sense of praise. Not just to the artist, but to the God who is so wildly generous in all of His gifts.

NOTES

1   H. Richard Niebuhr, *Christ and Culture* (New York: HarperCollins, 1986). I am adapting his paradigms, not adopting them exactly. I consider that his categories of "Christ above culture" and Christ transforming culture" are essentially the same.

2   Uwe Siemon-Netto, *The Fabricated Luther* (St. Louis: Concordia Publishing House, 1995).

3   Gene Edward Veith, *Modern Fascism: Liquidating the Judeo-Christian Worldview* (St. Louis: Concordia Publishing House, 1993), 56–77, 92–93.

4   For the orthodox Lutheran opposition to Hitler, see the life and writings of Hermann Sasse, who opposed the Nazis, had to flee to Australia, and was one of the greatest confessional Lutheran theologians of the 20th century.

5   Gustaf Wingren, *Luther on Vocation* (Evansville, IN: Ballast Press, 1994), 114.

6   See Wingren, 112.

7   Wingren, 123.

8   Quoted in Wingren, 123.

9   Martin Luther's "Treatise on Christian Liberty" [The Freedom of a Christian], in *Martin Luther: Selections from His Writings*, ed. John Dillenberger (New York: Anchor Books, 1961), 53.

CONCLUSION

WORSHIPING GOD

I remember when my wife and I first attended a Lutheran service. Coming as we did from liberal and evangelical backgrounds, we had never really experienced such a formal worship service. We liked it. It was different from what we were used to. We could tell that something significant was going on. So the next Sunday we came back. To our surprise, the congregation started chanting. This time, the service was not from a bulletin but from a red book, a sequence of prayers, scriptures, and ancient songs. The pastor, in robe and stole, was forgiving our sins and making the sign of the cross. The liturgy reached a crescendo with the sermon and peaked again with Holy Communion, in which the communicants knelt in adoration as the pastor placed the white wafer on their tongues. We felt like we had stepped into the Middle Ages.

It turned out, that first service that we had thought was so formal was that particular congregation's *informal* worship service. Once a month, they go casual. The rest of the time, they follow the traditional Lutheran liturgy. Since then, I have noticed that even when Lutherans try a less formal style of worship, they usually still end up being more formal than just about anyone else.

Lutheran spirituality is embodied, expressed tangibly, in Lutheran worship. In fact, though I have been discussing seemingly personal spiritual issues, such as justification and vocation, it is impossible to be Lutheran, really, without the church. Law and Gospel, the saving Word and Sacraments, the vocation of the pastor, and the Real Presence of Christ animate the liturgy at every point. Every week at worship, the Christian takes part in a divine drama, a mystery, in which Christ's gifts are received.

THE MYSTERY OF HOLINESS

After worshiping in that church for many months, I realized what was different about it. I was experiencing what I had never really known before, a sense of holiness. The robes, the rituals, the art, the music served to "set apart" what was happening from ordinary life. "Holiness" literally means "set apart," and in America at least, with our egalitarianism, casual ways, and laid-back attitudes, nothing is set apart and, as we say, nothing is sacred. But church, I was learning, was a place where something sacred could be found. The way the pastor would bow to the cross and to the Word of God on the altar, the way the congregation would rise and kneel, the majestic language of the liturgy convinced me that something different, something extraordinary is going on here.

And when the service culminated in Holy Communion the mystery of holiness became palpable. My wife and I knew we were not allowed to take Communion—we could not receive Christ's body until we had been thoroughly instructed, accepted into the fellowship, and knew what we were doing. Though all of the other churches we had attended, considering the sacrament not quite such a big deal, were free and easy about who could take Communion, I was not put off by the Lutherans' closed Communion practices and strict fellowship rules. Such practices were alien to my experience, but they added to the sense that something monumental was happening with the Sacrament. And to see the communicants go up to the altar, kneel, receive what they really believed to be, in the pastor's words, "the true body of Christ, given for you," and then come back to their pews, often with a transported, ecstatic expression on their faces—this drove home the point.

Many people tease Lutherans—and Lutherans tease themselves—about not worshiping in an emotional way. Indeed, Lutheran worship has an objective quality about it, the sense that grace is actually operating outside of one's own perceptions, that is very different from the more subjective styles favored by other theologies. Lutheran worship is God-centered, not human-centered. But I find Lutheran liturgical worship to be extraordinarily moving. It does make me emotional, not in the sense of some sort of spontaneous release, but in the sense of a powerful response to something real.

We found the services—and the depth of the preaching and the richness of the doctrines I started reading about—so compelling that we decided to join. This was not easy either. We waited several weeks before we realized there would be no altar call, no simple walk up to the front to "receive the right hand of fellowship" and thus become a member. We had to take a class that extended over months, as thorough and as long as the college courses I had just finished in graduate school, but there was a lot, a lot, to learn.

Finally, we were received into the community of the church. We received the Lord's Supper. Later, our newborn daughter was baptized. We were drawn further and further in.

HEAVEN ON EARTH

Lutheran worship bathes the congregation in the Word of God. The readings, the liturgical responses, the great set-pieces such as the Introit and the Kyrie, are not "vain repetitions," as our critics say. They are the very words of the Bible. Lutheran hymns are not emotional effusions. They are doctrinally and artistically rigorous explorations of a Biblical text. The creed and the prayers are grounded in Scripture. A Lutheran sermon is never a moralistic pep talk, nor a meditation on current events or pop psychology, but the proclamation of both Law and Gospel, drawn from the appointed text of Scripture. And Holy Communion is a reenactment of the Lord's Supper as recorded in the New Testament. The Word of God permeates Lutheran worship, and the Word of God is a means of grace.

The Australian theologian John Kleinig says that worship is nothing less than an experience of heaven on earth.[1] When earthly kingdoms try to build a heaven on earth, as we have said, the result is disaster; but the church, as part of the same spiritual kingdom that exists on earth as it is in heaven, brings heaven to earth every Sunday. What we do in worship is what the saints do in heaven; namely, come into the presence of God.

Drawing on biblical teachings about worship, from the temple through the Christ-centered worship of the new covenant (Hebrews 10 and 12), Pastor Kleinig maintains that when we worship in church, we are also worshiping along with the saints and the angels in heaven. Jesus, through His sacrifice, gives us complete access to God. Because we are in Christ, in God's eyes we are just as holy as Jesus is, and He hears all of our prayers, as if we were Jesus. So we can come into the Holy Place, into the presence of God—something that will happen in heaven and something that happens every Sunday.

We don't need to wait until we die, Pastor Kleinig says, to know how we stand with God. At the beginning of the worship service, we confess our sins, hear the Gospel, and are absolved of our sins. The pastor, in his vocation, is acting "in the stead and by the command of Christ," and so we hear Christ's judgment on us: Forgiven.

In the service of the Word, God addresses us through Scripture, and the Holy Spirit creates faith in our hearts. As we praise God in the hymns and psalms and glorias, we join with all Christians and all churches throughout the world—furthermore, with all the redeemed in heaven, from the ancient martyrs to our friends and relatives who are now with Christ.

Just as the Old Testament priests washed themselves in pure water, before they could enter the holy precincts of the temple, Christians have Baptism. Just as the Old Testament priests consecrated themselves with the blood of the sacrificial lamb, Christians receive Christ's blood in the Lord's Supper. And when Christ gives us His very body and blood in the bread and wine, He is really present, just as He is present in heaven and just as He was present to His disciples. In fact, says Pastor Kleinig, when we worship, Jesus is actually *more* accessible to us than He was to the disciples. He is closer to us, more intimately connected, since He has taken us into His cross.

The spirituality of the cross negates all moralism, but it inspires selfless service. The cross swallows up rationalistic speculation, while it affirms the truth of revelation in all of its ineffable mysteries. The cross counters the mere quest for mystical experience by lifting up what is inglorious, ordinary, even painful, yet, through the Word and Sacraments, offers a true union with Christ.

A spirituality in which God does everything for us may well seem too easy, too good to be true. There is, to be sure, nothing easy about being broken by the Law, struggling against one's own nature, and fighting through trials and suffering. But, on another level, it is indeed easy, simply a matter of receiving Christ's gifts. And the Gospel of forgiveness and grace in the cross, is, as the catechism says, "most certainly true." This truth is no mere intellectual assertion, but a faith lived out in worship, in the inmost depths of the heart, in love of others, in work, and in the day-to-day routines of ordinary life.

NOTES

[1] What I learned from Pastor Kleinig came from a presentation he made when he was in this country at Elm Grove Lutheran Church, in Elm Grove, Wisconsin.

appeNδix

THE FIRST EVANGELICALS

AND OTHER CHURCHES

This is an article I wrote for Touchstone: A Journal of Mere Christianity *(May/June 1998):14–17, under the rather formidable title "Evangelical Catholics and Confessional Evangelicals: The Ecumenical Polarities of Lutheranism."*

It positions Lutheranism with other Christian traditions, gives some background about the Lutheran church today, and offers some other explanations that may prove helpful. I had thought to work this material into the book, but its tone and approach is somewhat different, and it seems to me that it works best as a self-contained article. So here I offer it for what it is worth.

Imagine a church that is both evangelical—proclaiming the free forgiveness of sins through faith in Jesus Christ—and sacramental, centering its spiritual life in the regenerating waters of baptism and the real presence of Christ in Holy Communion. Imagine further a church that is strongly grounded on Scripture, but yet avoids the solipsism of individual interpretation in favor of a comprehensive, intellectually rigorous and imminently orthodox theological system. Imagine a worship service that features both strong preaching *and* the historic liturgy. Imagine that this is a historical church with a rich spiritual tradition, but without legalism. Imagine, in short, a church that has some of the best parts of Protestantism and the best parts of Catholicism. Finally, imagine that this church body is not some little made-up sect, but one of the largest bodies of Christians in the world.

Such a church might seem like what many Christians, disaffected by both the vacuity of liberal theology and the shallowness of American evangelicalism, are dreaming of. Such a church exists. It goes by the admittedly inadequate name "Lutheran."

Worldwide, there are some 60,000,000 Lutherans on the books, making it the largest Protestant tradition of them all. There are around 9 million Lutherans in the United States, but five million in Africa and another five million in Asia. Brazil has over a million, and it is one of the dominant religions of Papua New Guinea. In the United States, there are about the same number of *Missouri Synod* Lutherans (2.5 million) as there are Episcopalians.

And yet, the Lutheran church seems almost unknown in American Christianity. Catholics, Episcopalians, Baptists, charismatics, and Calvinists are well represented in theological debates, opinion polls, and articles in Christian publications, but Lutherans—who have their own distinctive approach to everything from salvation to politics—are often theological wallflowers.

Billy Graham called Lutherans "the sleeping giant." If Lutheranism is the invisible church, or, to paraphrase what Luther said of God, the church that hides itself, this is partly its own fault and partly the result of its theological tension with American culture. Nevertheless, Lutheranism has much to offer Christendom as a whole. As a church body with a thoroughly worked-out theology, which it actually follows, some Lutheran denominations have retained their orthodoxy more successfully than most. But more than that, Lutheran theology—and spirituality—is animated by a dynamic polarity in which divisive theological controversies are put into balance and thus resolved.

PARADOXY

The distinctive characteristic of Lutheran theology is its affirmation of paradox. Calvin and Arminius both constructed systematic theologies, explaining away any contrary biblical data in a rationalistic system of belief. Luther developed his theology in Bible commentaries, following the contours of Scripture wherever they lead and developing its most profound polarities: Law and Gospel; Christ as both true God and true Man; the Christian as simultaneously saint and sinner; justification by faith and baptismal regeneration; Holy Communion as the real presence of Christ in material bread and wine.

Not only have Lutherans always affirmed both "evangelical" and "Catholic" ideas, their way with paradox also resolves issues that have divided Protestants. Calvinists insist on salvation by grace alone to the extent of double predestination; Arminians insist that everyone, potentially, can be saved, and so stress the utter freedom of the will. Lutherans stress grace above all, that God does literally everything for our salvation, dying on the Cross, with His Spirit breaking into our lives through Word and Sacrament, the means of grace. But Jesus died for all, and potentially anyone might be saved. Lutheranism affirms the best of both Calvinism and Arminianism, while avoiding the exclusivity of the one and the potential Pelagianism of the other. Charismatics emphasize the Holy Spirit—so do Lutherans, finding that Spirit not in the vagaries of human emotion but even more tangibly as being genuinely operative in the Word and Sacraments. Lutherans are tenacious in their doctrinal rigor, while excluding separatism and legalism. Lutheran cultural theology affirms *two kingdoms*, preventing the secular from swallowing up the sacred, and the sacred from swallowing up the secular. (This explains why Lutherans can seem both inwardly focused and free and easy, why they seem conservative yet apolitical, and why they often have beer at their church dinners.)

Lutheranism—with its sacramentalism and liturgical worship synthesized with its biblical emphasis and evangelical proclamation—might serve as a bridge among the various factions of Christianity. Of course, it is not that simple.

If Lutheranism represents an "evangelical Catholicism" (a term favored by many confessional Lutherans), its paradoxes mean that it is likewise subject to attack from every side. Evangelicals consider Lutheranism "too Catholic," making fun of what they consider its stiff formality, its old-fashioned music, and ancient liturgy and, more seriously, questioning how Lutherans can say salvation is by faith if they believe in baptismal regeneration and being appalled at the way the pastor says, when he gives the absolution, that he forgives people their sins. Catholics (and Orthodox) lump Lutheranism with all other Protestants—in fact, Lutherans are the worst because they started the "dissolution" of Christendom.

Within Protestantism, Calvinists attack Lutherans for "not going far enough in the Reformation," for keeping papistical practices and idolatrous worship. Arminians attack Lutherans for not believing in the freedom of the will and for leaving the door open to antinomianism. Charismatics think Lutherans are "cold." Fundamentalists say Lutherans are strong on doctrine but weak on morals.

And, just as the Lutheran framework invites attacks from every side, Lutherans find themselves counterattacking against everyone else. Lutherans condemn Arminians for not believing in predestination and Calvinists for believing in double predestination. Catholics and charismatics are considered alike in believing that the Holy Spirit reveals Himself in human beings, apart from the Word. Fundamentalists are savaged for their legalism. In fact, many Lutherans do not see themselves as being Protestant at all.

The fact is, the Lutheran synthesis is a baroque structure that can only be held together by a doctrinal rigor that constantly reinforces every point. Anglicans attempt a *via media* between Catholicism and Protestantism, which works through compromise, broad consensus, and a tolerance for differences. The Lutheran way, on the other hand, is one of polarities. Each pole of the paradox must be maintained and heightened. What Chesterton said in *Orthodoxy* of the paradoxes of Christianity is particularly descriptive of Lutheran theology: "We want not an amalgam or compromise, but both things at the top of their energy; love and wrath both burning." Christianity does not approach doctrinal issues such as the nature of Christ or the moral status of a human being in terms of the Aristotelian golden mean. Rather, "Christianity got over the difficulty of combining furious opposites, by keeping them both, and keeping them both furious."

Thus, Lutherans are *very* sacramental and *very* evangelical. Anglicanism, even in its High-Church phase, has always been dismissed by continental Lutherans as merely another variety of Reformed Calvinism, its articles being too wishy-washy in not clearly affirming the Real Presence. Evangelicals are not evangelical enough, falling as they do into the trap of "decision theology" and moralism, not trusting God to accomplish literally everything that is needful.

As a result, Lutheran theology, though embracing in one sense the whole range of Christian spirituality, is nevertheless an entity unto itself, with its own spiritual disciplines that are quite alien to those of other traditions. Consider, for example, the way Lutheranism opposes the so-called *theology* (or rather, spirituality) *of glory*—with its pretensions of power, victory, and earthly success—with the *theology of the cross*, in which God reveals Himself in weakness, defeat, and failure. Or the Word of God, not merely as a sourcebook of information, but as a sacramental means of grace. Or the way God hides Himself in what seems to be His opposite, in the material elements of the sacraments, in humiliation and defeat, in what seems most secular and nonreligious. Or the exhilaration, under the Gospel, of Christian freedom.

LUTHERANISM IN AMERICAN CULTURE

An immigrant faith, like Catholicism and Orthodoxy, Lutheran churches had always been somewhat culturally isolated and highly conscious of their differences with mainstream American Protestantism. While German Lutherans came to Pennsylvania in colonial times and Scandinavian Lutherans settled in the upper midwest, bringing their churches with them, another group came for a different reason.

In 19th century Germany, efforts were being made by the post-Enlightenment princes to combine the various Protestant factions into a single, ecumenical, state church. Calvinists and Lutherans were forced to give up their doctrinal distinctiveness and combine into an "Evangelical and Reformed" church. ("Evangelical"—referring to the centrality of the Gospel—is the preferred continental term for Lutheranism, as opposed to the "Reformed" Calvinists. Lutherans were thus the first, and one might argue, the quintessential evangelicals.) The state churches so formed tended to be rationalistic, cultural religions—preaching new agricultural techniques and doctrines of social progress rather than the Gospel—the fruit of the new liberal theology being developed in German seminaries. In the typical heavy-handed German way, pastors who opposed the ecumenical union were actually imprisoned and the so-called "Old Lutherans" were persecuted. Scores of congregations that insisted on classical Lutheranism left everything they owned and settled in America. (Substantial numbers also went to other countries such as Australia, Africa, and Brazil.)

These formed the more conservative Lutheran denominations, such as the Missouri Synod and the Wisconsin Synod (terms that refer to the place of their historical origins and denominational headquarters), churches that, because of their history, would naturally be suspicious of ecumenism. Like the Catholics, these confessional Lutherans, recognizing that the Protestant civil religion of the public schools was inimical to their faith, established an extensive system of parochial schools to educate their children in a way that would be supportive of their faith. This strain of Lutherans thus resisted assimilation into the mainstream of American religious life. In terms of their *two kingdoms* theology, they assimilated quite well into American society and economic life, but their church was kept separate, untouched by the revivalism, the social gospel, religious individualism, and other trends of American religion.

But if one tendency in American Lutheranism is a certain separatism, the other part of the inevitable polarity is accomodationism. The colonial-era Lutherans and many of the Scandinavian settlers were not so strict as the religious refugee-Lutherans. Quite early, these Lutherans debated about to what extent they should adapt to the religious life of their new homeland. An important 19th-century theologian, Samuel Schmucker, went so far as to amend the Augsburg Confession to accommodate the new revivalism and a more Reformed view of the sacraments. While many Lutherans went in this direction, another theologian, Charles Krauth, in a movement paralleling the Oxford movement within Anglicanism, championed a revival of confessionalism and liturgical renewal.

Ever since, American Lutherans have tended to vacillate between the poles of separatism and accomodationism. Historically, Lutheran denominations in America have tended to drift towards the religious mainstream, only to lurch back into their distinctiveness.

In this century, The Lutheran Church—Missouri Synod (LCMS) has gone through a particularly traumatic civil war. Its seminary in St. Louis gradually began accepting the approach to the Scripture of other mainline protestant denominations, employing the historical-critical method to cast doubt on the authority of the Bible and adopting other tenets of liberal theology. In the 1970s, "the battle of the Bible" erupted, when conservatives called to task "the moderates," who held an unorthodox view of the Scriptures. The latter walked out, set up a seminary of their own, and every congregation had to choose which side they would be on. Unlike what happened in other denominations, the liberals left and the conservatives retained control of the institution (rather than the conservatives leaving, which has usually been the case in other church bodies).

Today, the LCMS is facing a similar issue again, only now the American religious mainstream is no longer liberalism but evangelicalism. Many Lutheran churches have been jettisoning their liturgy and their distinctive beliefs, in favor of emulating the evangelicals, adapting techniques from the church growth movement, singing "praise songs," preaching sermons on pop-psychology, and otherwise abandoning their spiritual heritage in favor of generic American Protestantism.

In the meantime, the moderate exodus from the LCMS served as the catalyst for the union of the nation's more liberal Lutherans. The resulting Evangelical Lutheran Church of America (ELCA) continued going the way of the rest of mainline Protestantism. The ordination of women, leftwing political advocacy, and the ecumenical movement have made them less distinctive, and more and more like generic American liberal Protestantism.

In some places, genuine Lutheranism—despite all of the Lutheran churches—has become hard to find. But, as it always has, the pendulum may be starting to swing in the other direction.

LUTHERAN CONFESSIONALISM

Today, a new confessionalism is emerging in Lutheran circles. Just as many Lutheran churches are going the way of American evangelicalism in using praise bands and overhead projectors, others are reemphasizing the historic liturgy, chanting the service and signing themselves with the holy cross. Many parishes have re-instituted the ancient Lutheran practice of private confession and absolution.

The most rigorously confessional Lutheran pastors can be recognized by their black shirts and white clerical collars, the priest-like garb worn by traditional holders of the pastoral office before they adopted the American-style minister's coat and tie. (All Lutheran pastors have the collar; the archconfessionalists are distinguished by wearing it practically all the time.)

This confessionalism can appear formidable. Closed communion (sharing the Lord's Supper only with those who are agreed on every point of doctrine), a genuine pastoral authority, rigorous catechetical instruction for converts, and forthright practices (such as no weddings during Lent, and no congratulatory eulogies during funerals), can be off-putting in America's easy-going culture. But confessionalism is not the same as conservatism. (During the LCMS controversy over the Bible, "high church" ceremonialists tended to be on the liberal side; today, while theologically orthodox, they stand against the evangelical and fundamentalist tendencies within the church.)

Lutherans allow a measure of freedom in practice, while insisting on agreement in doctrine (unlike, say, the Anglican tradition which has tended to stress on uniformity of worship forms while allowing for doctrinal latitude). Conservative denominations such as the Missouri and Wisconsin Synods remain rigorously "confessional," in the sense of upholding the creeds and formulas of the Book of Concord, though they are presently torn by controversies over worship styles. That style is expressive of confession, though, is becoming more and more evident, and serious fault lines seem to be manifesting themselves within the conservative Lutheran denominations. Most Lutherans today are somewhere along the spectrum between the two poles of low church informality and high church ceremonialism.

Nevertheless, it is surely significant that many of the most ardently confessional pastors, those who are most concerned to bring back the Lutheran traditions in both doctrine and worship, are those straight out of seminary. The younger pastors, the new generation, seem to be the ones most concerned to recover their Lutheran distinctives.

In the meantime, Lutherans are starting to get their share of disaffected evangelicals—casualties of megachurches and refugees from generic American Protestantism, Christians looking for meaningful worship and theological depth—as well as Catholics dismayed by the post-Vatican II liberalism within their church, and burnt-out secularists who, broken by the Law and renewed by the Gospel, have come to Christ.

Confessional Lutherans are not ecumenical. They will never join the National Association of Evangelicals, nor the World Council of Churches. Lutheran institutions are so big—with their network of schools, colleges, publishing houses, and denominational services—that they can be rather insulated and self-contained. Though the ELCA has pioneered ecumenical dialogue with the Reformed, Anglicans, and even Catholicism—to the point of claiming to have found agreement with Rome on justification by faith—the Missouri and Wisconsin Synods will have none of that. (It should be emphasized that there is also a growing confessional movement within the ELCA, often in conflict with the institutional bureaucracy.) The Lutheran wariness of ecumenical union and, even more profoundly, of American-style Christianity have kept them out of the mainstream, but it has kept them relatively true to their theology.

Any genuine ecumenism must avoid simply emptying Christianity of its distinctive content and must somehow affirm what is most salient, what is most "Christian," in the whole spectrum of Christian belief, from traditional Catholicism to Protestant fundamentalism. Lutheranism, while eschewing ecumenism as such, provides a framework—or, rather, a set of polarities—by which this might be done.

Many confessional Lutherans have taken to calling themselves "evangelical catholics." They are catholic in their historical creeds, their worship, and their sacramentalism, and they are evangelical in their trust in the good news of Christ, that in His cross He has saved us by sheer grace for a life of Christian freedom.

Others are calling themselves "confessing evangelicals," allying with Reformed Christians to call today's doctrinally shallow evangelicals to the historic confessions of faith forged by the Reformation. From the Lutheran perspective, pure Catholics are in need of evangelical reformation, and pure evangelicals are in need of historical orthodoxy. The theological formulas that purport to show how both of these tasks can be done are collected in a volume appropriately titled *The Book of Concord*.

FOR FURTHER READING

This book has barely scratched the surface of Lutheran spirituality. Here are just a few books for those who would like to go deeper into the subject. Of course, the best treatment of Lutheran theology can be found in the writings of Martin Luther, who is both a profound theologian and a brilliant writer. His works are never academic, abstract theologizing, but personal and deeply devotional meditations—filled sometimes with invective to be sure, but also humor, honest accounts of his own struggles, and piercing insights into Scripture. Good starting points would be his Bible commentaries, such as those on Galatians and Romans.

Another primary source is the collection of Lutheran creeds and confessions known as *The Book of Concord*. Particularly useful is Luther's Large Catechism and the basic, though inexhaustible primer of Lutheran instruction, the Small Catechism.

In addition, here are some books that have shaped this book and my own understanding. Any pastor could direct you to more, and himself would be a valuable resource:

C. F. W. Walther, *The Proper Distinction Between Law and Gospel*. Trans. W. H. T. Dau. St. Louis: Concordia Publishing House, 1986. A father of American Lutheranism in the 19th century and a founder of the Missouri Synod, Walther also wrote this classic exposition of this characteristic Lutheran distinction that is not just theological scholarship but makes for fine devotional reading.

John Theodore Mueller, *Christian Dogmatics*. St. Louis: Concordia Publishing House, 1951. Here are the prooftexts, the arguments, the controversies, and the systematic treatments neglected in my own book, but important in their own right. Mueller draws on the even more exhaustive treatments found in the multi-volume dogmatics by Francis Pieper.

Walter von Loewenich, *Luther's Theology of the Cross*. Trans. Herbert J. A. Bouman. Minneapolis: Augsburg, 1976. A rich overview of a rich doctrine, of which a number of other valuable books have also been written.

Richard C. Eyer. *Pastoral Care Under the Cross: God in the Midst of Suffering*. St. Louis: Concordia Publishing House, 1994. A hospital chaplain—and now my colleague and friend—applies the theology of the cross to the realities of human suffering.

Senkbeil, Harold. *Sanctification: Christ in Action*. Milwaukee: Northwestern Publishing House, 1989. A lucid contrast between Lutheranism and typical American evangelicalism.

———. *Dying to Live*. St. Louis: Concordia Publishing House, 1997. A meditation on the church year, the liturgy, and the Word and Sacraments by a pastor who has become one of my mentors.

Koeberle, Adolf. *The Quest for Holiness*. Trans. John C. Mattes. Minneapolis: Augsburg, 1938; reprinted, Evansville, IN: Ballast Press, 1995. George Strieter, a Lutheran layman, is performing the inestimable service of reprinting spiritual classics that have gone out of print and have become hard to find. This account of the spiritual life is unutterably profound. Order it from Ballast Press, P.O. Box 1193, Evansville, IN 47706-1193. Or call Mr. Strieter's business at 1-800-335-4672.

Wingren, Gustaf. *Luther on Vocation*. Trans. Carl C. Rasmussen. Minneapolis: Augsburg; reprinted, Evansville, IN: Ballast Press, 1994. A book that is not merely about work, but about the

Christian life. This book can transform the way you look at ordinary life. Order it from Ballast Press, P.O. Box 1193, Evansville, IN 47706-1193. Or call Mr. Strieter's business at 1-800-335-4672.

Gerhard, Johann. *Sacred Meditations*. Decatur, IL: Repristination Press, 1998. Profound devotions, classics of Lutheran spirituality, first published in 1606 by a 22-year-old theologian. Repristination Press, 3555 Plover Drive, Decatur, IL 62526; e-mail: *HUNNIUS@aol.com* reprints Lutheran classics.

Sasse, Hermann. *We Confess*. 3 vols. Trans. Norman Nagel. St. Louis: Concordia Publishing House, 1984–1986. These three short booklets—on *Jesus Christ, The Sacraments,* and *The Church*—are a good introduction to the writings of a theologian who stood up against Hitler and who articulated his faith without compromise in the context of modern times. Sasse's writings are profound and theologically rich, but they are also devotional, works of spiritual reflection.

Giertz, Bo. *The Hammer of God: A Novel About the Cure of Souls*. Trans. Clifford Ansgar Nelson. Minneapolis: Augsburg, 1960. This novel, by a confessional Swedish bishop, dramatizes the dynamics of Lutheran spirituality as it is lived out in everyday life. It follows three generations of Lutheran pastors, who must deal with the alternative spiritualities of pietism and modernism in their own lives and ministry to others, until they rediscover the radical Gospel of the cross.

Gene edward veith, jr., is Professor of English at Concordia University-Wisconsin, Mequon, WI.

Born in Alva, OK, Veith holds a B.A. in Letters with Distinction from the University of Oklahoma (1972), a M.A. in English from the University of Kansas (1975), and a Ph.D. in English from the University of Kansas (1979).

Dr. Veith is the author of *Post-Modern Times, Modern Fascism: Liquidation of the Judeo-Christian Worldview, Reading between the Lines, Loving God with All Your Mind, The Gift of Art, The Place of the Arts in Scripture, Reformation Spirituality: The Religion of George Herbert,* and numerous articles and book reviews. He is the culture editor for *World* magazine and writes a weekly column.

Dr. Veith and his wife, Jackquelyn, have three children, Paul, Joanna, and Mary.